728.5

STEVE DOBSON

UNUSUAL HOTELS

EUROPE

JonGlez

INTRODUCTION

Far from seeking out luxury or charming hotels that are often inaccessible to ordinary mortals because they are prohibitively expensive and then turn out to be soulless, unwelcoming places, the "Unusual Hotels - Europe" guide lists 150 hotels with exceptional features, astonishingly original and out of the ordinary.

We've taken great pleasure in carefully choosing hotels with extremely high standards that know how to surprise you with their utter uniqueness. Catering for all budgets (from 20 euros to over 1,000 euros per night), the places alone are very often worth the trip and will certainly make your stay unforgettable.

We sincerely hope that you'll enjoy visiting them as much as we did! Bon voyage!

Our selection criteria
Properties do not pay a fee to be included in this book and are selected by the editorial team.

Submit your suggestions
Comments on this book and its contents, as well as information on places we may not have mentioned, are more than welcome and will enrich future editions.
Don't hesitate to contact us:
• Jonglez publishing, 17, boulevard du Roi, 78000 Versailles, France
• E-mail: info@jonglezpublishing.com

Reykjavik

ICELAND

ARCTIC OCEAN

Tromsø   Murmansk

Ivalo

Rovaniemi

Luleå   Tornio
              Oulu   RUSSIA

FAROE
ISLANDS   Umeå   FINLAND   Kuopio
                    Östersund   Vaasa
                                                    Tampere

                Bergen   Sundsvall   St.
                     NORWAY   SWEDEN   Petersburg
                                                   Helsinki
                  Stavanger Oslo   Tallinn
                         Drammen   Stockholm   ESTONIA   Novgorod
Inverness   Göteborg   Pskov
                NORTH   Riga   RUSSIA
        Aberdeen SEA   Aalborg Jönköping LATVIA
Londonderry Glasgow Edinburgh DENMARK   LITHUANIA Vicebsk
    Belfast   Aarhus   BALTIC   Vilnius
IRELAND Douglas Newcastle Odense København   SEA   Minsk
              Upon-Tyne   Kaliningrad Kaunas
Limerick Dublin Kiel   RUSSIA   Gdańsk   BELARUS
    Cork   Manchester NETHERLANDS Hamburg Olsztyn
        Birmingham Amsterdam Bremen Berlin POLAND
UNITED   Hannover Poznań Warszawa
Cardiff KINGDOM Rotterdam Essen   Lublin
    Bristol London Köln Dresden Wrocław   UKRAINE
        Dover Brussels Liège Erfurt Katowice L'viv
ENGLISH CHANNEL Lille BELGIUM GERMANY Praha Kraków Košice
Brest Rouen Luxembourg Nürnberg CZECH Ostrava
    Caen Reims Metz   REPUBLIC Brno SLOVAKIA
Rennes Paris Nancy Strasbourg München Wien Bratislava Debrecen MOLDOVA
NORTH ATLANTIC Le Mans Troyes Salzburg Budapest Cluj-Napoca
OCEAN Nantes Bourges Basel Vaduz AUSTRIA HUNGARY Oradea ROMANIA
        FRANCE Bern LIECHTENSTEIN Ljubljana SLOVENIA Zagreb Bucuresti
La Coruña Limoges Genève Zürich Verona Venezia CROATIA Beograd
    Bilbao Clermont- SWITZERLAND Milano   Zadar
Ortia Bayonne Ferrand Lyon Torino Modena Ravenna BOSNIA AND SERBIA BULGARIA
Valladolid Bordeaux   Firenze HERZEGOVINA Sarajevo Sofia
Salamanca Zaragoza Toulouse Montpellier Monaco San Marino MONTENEGRO Plovdiv
Coimbra Madrid Barcelona Marseille Corse Roma ITALY Pescara Podgorica Skopje Edirne
Lisboa SPAIN   Islas   Bari ALBANIA MACEDONIA
PORTUGAL Valencia Baleares Sardegna Napoli Tiranë Thessaloniki
Sevilla Granada Alicante   MEDITERRANEAN SEA Taranto Lárissa
Cádiz Málaga   Palermo Messina GREECE Pátra
                         Reggio di   Athina
                         Calabria
                         Catania
                  MALTA
                    Valletta   Crete

AFRICA

0 100 200 300 400 km

CONTENTS

UNITED KIGNDOM

BELGIUM AND NETHERLANDS

FRANCE

SPAIN AND PORTUGAL

ITALY AND REST OF EUROPE

GERMANY, AUSTRIA AND SWITZERLAND

SCANDINAVIA

UNITED KINGDOM

NICOLLE TOWER

Navigation tower and lookout

NICOLLE TOWER ❶
St Clement's, Jersey

THE LANDMARK TRUST
Shottesbrooke
Maidenhead
Berkshire SL6 3SW
01628 825925
bookings@landmarktrust.org.uk
www.landmarktrust.org.uk

ROOMS AND RATES
With a single bedroom
for two, this cosy
landmark offers a unique
perspective of the island
and its surroundings.
Prices for the whole property
are from £135 for a four
night midweek break in
January, to £1042 for a
week in July/August.
The staircase is necessarily
steep without access for
disabled guests. The tower
also provides a garden should
you tire of bird's-eye views.

This 160 ft navigational mark is located in a field called Le Clos de Hercanty, where Hercanty means "tilted menhir". Used as a navigation mark, a small rectangular lookout was built next to the stone. In 1644, this half-buried slab of diorite was marked with a compass rose inscription to become part of the foundations of a new lookout building, forming one corner. Records indicate that 18th-century owner Philippe Nicolle added the octagonal sitting room on the first floor in 1821. Further work was undertaken in 1943 by the occupying forces of the German army. They made an observation or control position here by astutely raising the roof of the octagon by a single storey so that no change would be noticed from the air. Although this latest addition with its slit eyes and German ranging marks on its thick concrete ceiling isn't part of the original tower, it has been renovated as part of the tower's history.

TO DO
Set back from the coast, 160 ft up, the tower provides endlessly fascinating views over the sea and island in every direction.

VISITOR COMMENTS
• *Peace, lovely walks, our own tower to live in – what more could you want?*

THE EGYPTIAN HOUSE

Celebration of Napoleonic success in Egypt

THE EGYPTIAN HOUSE **❷**
Chapel Street,
Penzance, Cornwall

THE LANDMARK TRUST
Shottesbrooke
Maidenhead
Berkshire SL6 3SW
01628 825925
bookings@landmarktrust.org.uk
www.landmarktrust.org.uk

ROOMS AND RATES
Three apartments. The
first floor with a narrow
oval staircase to negotiate
accommodates up to three.
The second and third floors
accommodate up to four each
in double and twin rooms.
Prices for the whole
property are from £162 for
a four-night midweek break
in January, to £719 for a
week in July / August.

Of a style in vogue after Napoleon's campaign in Egypt of 1798, the Egyptian House dates from about 1835. The front elevation is very similar to that of the former Egyptian Hall in Piccadilly, designed in 1812 by P. F. Robinson. Robinson or Foulston of Plymouth are the most likely candidates for its design, although there is no evidence to support the claim of either. It was built for John Lavin as a museum and geological repository. Bought by The Landmark Trust in 1968, its colossal façade, with lotus-bud capitals and enrichments of Coade stone, concealed two small granite houses above shops, solid and with a pleasant rear elevation, but very decrepit inside. These were reconstructed into three compact apartments, the highest of which has a view through a small window of Mounts Bay and St Michael's Mount, over the chimney pots of the city.

VISITOR COMMENTS

• *No photograph or drawing can depict the astonishing and eccentric elevation of the Egyptian house.*

• *We much appreciated the furniture and delighted in the witty Egyptian motifs.*

LUNDY ISLAND

A preserved castle, lighthouse and cottages on this nature reserve island

LUNDY ISLAND ❸
Bristol Channel, Devon

THE LANDMARK TRUST
Shottesbrooke
Maidenhead
Berkshire SL6 3SW
01628 825925
bookings@landmarktrust.org.uk
www.landmarktrust.org.uk

ROOMS AND RATES
There are a variety of
overnight options including
cottages, a hostel and even
camping. The twenty-three
houses and cottages include
some built around the keep
of the castle, the keeper's
quarters of the lighthouse
and a stone refuge without
electricity – "Tibbets", which
has its own rustic charm.
Between March and
November, The Landmark
Trust runs a ferry from
Bideford or Ilfracombe
carrying day and overnight
visitors, weather permitting.
Autumn and winter access
is by helicopter from
Hartland Point. Prices
vary according to the type
of accommodation.

Lundy ("Puffin Island"), in the approaches to the Bristol Channel, is 3 miles long and rises over 400 ft out of the sea, commanding a tremendous view of England, Wales and the Atlantic. It has tall cliffs towards the south and west, with grass and heather on top, and steep side lands with trees, shrubs and bracken in small hanging valleys, rich in wildflowers, on the east coast facing the mainland. There are three lighthouses (two in use), a castle, a church, a working farm, a pub, several handsome houses and cottages, and a population of about eighteen. Most of the buildings and all the field walls are made from the island's beautiful light-coloured granite.

When Lundy was taken on by The National Trust in 1969 (thanks mainly to the generosity of Sir Jack Hayward), The Landmark Trust undertook the restoration and running of the island. The formidable task of tidying up and restoring the buildings and services for both visitors and residents took them over twenty years. Much of this work remains invisible, but without it ordinary people would soon have been unable to live on or visit the island.

VINTAGE VACATIONS

Vintage Airstream caravans – restored and adored

VINTAGE VACATIONS ❹
Near Newport
Isle of Wight
07802 758113
anything@
vintagevacations.co.uk
www.vintagevacations.co.uk

LOCATION AND RATES
Newport is a 10
minute drive away.
2011 weekly bookings in
high summer are £625
for a trailer of up to four
guests, with reduced rates
for low season, midweek
and 2 night weekend breaks,
which are from only £175.
Gas, water, electricity,
towels and all linen are
included. Now with ten
caravans on offer, the
site books up quickly.
To preserve these works
of art, the caravans are
non-smoking throughout and
pets are not admitted on site.

Starting with a single Airstream caravan bought on eBay in 2004 as a weekend escape from London, Helen Cunningham saw the opportunity to offer these icons of travelling hospitality to others. Located on a working farm campsite, the first of these 60s and 70s works of aluminium art were brought to the Isle of Wight from Missouri and enhanced with a treasure trove of furnishings and period decor from Helen's stylist background. From melamine plates to retro print fabrics, Helen and partner Frazer have shared a stockpile of period artefacts to make the Vintage Vacation experience a hazy trip down memory lane – full of a sense of period fun.

Modern conveniences such as fridges and CD players are hidden behind the vintage exteriors so you can enjoy yourself without sacrifice. They even include a hairdryer and toaster! Some of the larger models have enough space for travel cots. The campsite has a beach hut with proper toilet facilities as you can't use the toilets on board. Once inside your Airstream you'll easily understand why they are still considered king of the road for luxury camping.

Caravans sleep up to four, however vintage folding caravans are available to hire on site for noisy children or larger families. Helen notes that guests are "More bohemian than bog standard".

To keep everything as original as possible, Vintage Vacations have stayed with the USA voltage. This means that each trailer has its own transformer to convert UK power supply to US. There is a travel adaptor on board. Some devices such as iPods and certain DVD players and phone chargers will work, but not all, so bring a couple of favourite CDs just in case.

LUTTRELL'S TOWER

Georgian tower with views of the Solent and smugglers access tunnel

LUTTRELL'S TOWER ❺
Eaglehurst, Southampton,
Hampshire

THE LANDMARK TRUST
Shottesbrooke
Maidenhead
Berkshire SL6 3SW
01628 825925
bookings@landmarktrust.org.uk
www.landmarktrust.org.uk

ROOMS AND RATES
Accommodation for up to
four in a double and twin
bedroom combination.
Prices for the whole
property are from £562
for a four-night midweek
break in January to £2,765
for a week in July/August.

This Georgian folly, possibly the only surviving work of Thomas Sandby, first professor of architecture at the Royal Academy, stands on the shore of the Solent looking towards Cowes. The view, particularly of ships entering and leaving Southampton by the deep-water channel, is endlessly fascinating. Giant ships, sailing and pleasure craft of all shapes and sizes travel along this busy waterway and home of sailing. The view from the windows opposite the Fawley refinery and power station is in its own way equally impressive, with miles of complex pipework knitted together in an intricate sculpture.

The tower was built for Temple Luttrell, an MP who gained a reputation locally as a smuggler, perhaps because of a tunnel running from the basement to the beach. His brother-in-law, Lord Cavan, who commanded British forces in Egypt from 1801, was the next owner and brought with him the two mysterious feet on a plinth of Nubian granite, now at the tower and thought to be the base of a XIXth dynasty statue of Rameses II. The tower had several owners, including for a time Marconi, who used it for his wireless experiments of 1912.

Purchased by The Landmark Trust in 1968 and restored to its former splendour, all the rooms have handsome chimney-pieces and the top room has fine plaster and shellwork as well. This top room has been arranged with an open-plan kitchen so that you can cook, eat and relax in it, watching the Solent all the while.

CRAZY BEAR – OXFORD

Flamboyance and extravagance in a country setting

CRAZY BEAR HOTEL ⑥
Bear Lane
Stadhampton
Oxfordshire OX44 7UR
01865 890714
enquiries@crazybear-
oxford.co.uk
www.crazybeargroup.co.uk

RATES AND LOCATION
Seventeen rooms with
doubles from £150 per room
per night and suites up to
£345 excluding tax. The
hotel is down country lanes
on the outskirts of Oxford,
which is only an hour from
London or Birmingham.

This was no ordinary pub conversion! Reception is a lavishly restyled London Routemaster double-decker bus, so you know you're in for something different from the outset.

Tropical gardens lead you to the heart of the hotel – originally a 16th-century building that has been bravely redesigned to house the charismatic bar with its 8 ft bear in a chandeliered gallery. Garden paths wander past a waterfall, dense palm trees, terraces, lawns and eye-catching art scattered throughout the grounds.

A total of seventeen individually designed bedrooms, suites and cottages showcase amazing creativity and charisma, with real wow-factor. Elaborate furniture, mirrors and beautifully crafted, sumptuous leather provide eclectic drama. The cottages can cater for families and groups of up to six, while the suites and rooms are more in keeping with a luxury romantic break for two.

Award-winning dining is another feature of the hotel. From the vibrant bar, you walk past the bear down to a Thai brasserie in a dramatic haven of its own. Royal Thai cuisine is prepared using produce from the hotel's farm and direct from Thailand. Equally sumptuous, the English restaurant envelops you in padded leather and offers modern British food.

Private dinners, weddings and meetings can take place in a rich oak room, a garden log cabin or a huge Moroccan glasshouse that opens to terraces, croquet lawn and a private copse. All of this is set at the front of 60 acres of farmland, home to rare breed animals and The Crazy Bear Farm Shop which rears, butchers, cures and smokes its own produce for the hotel.

CRAZY BEAR HOTEL – BEACONSFIELD

Luxury design at its most dramatic

THE CRAZY BEAR ❼
Old Beaconsfield
Bucks HP9 1LX
01494 673086
enquiries@crazybear-
beaconsfield.co.uk
www.crazybeargroup.co.uk

ROOMS AND RATES
Ten suites from £345 -
£430 excluding tax

LOCATION
Just off the M40 motorway,
about 30 minutes from
central London or Heathrow.

The oldest documented building in Beaconsfield has been magnificently restored over four years in a made-to-order, without restraint, makeover. Its redesign can only be described as awesome – dramatic architecture, luxurious materials, spectacular lighting and even an underground extension create an elaborate, luxurious property.

Each of the ten individually designed bedrooms uses materials to dramatic effect. Textured leather, suede, oak, porcelain, velvet and lots of gold leaf decorate rooms which are themselves filled with statement furniture and theatrical ornamentation.

The main bar is a work of art in its own right. From an Italian jade marble floor and gloss-polished walnut and copper bar, to the two huge skylights where a row of six 1930s crystal chandeliers sit, all is top-to-toe luxury. Along one wall is a custom-made, 55 ft black Chesterfield, studded with Swarovski crystals. There are polished pewter tables and stools. Heavy crushed-velvet curtains drape from antique hand-carved oak panelling to complete the extreme decor.

A grand white marble staircase with an elaborate ironwork vine sculpture and python banister leads to the private bar, The Crystal Room. This underground Aladdin's cave has mirrored walls, ceiling and fibre-optic lighting effects, and is tastefully furnished with lots of pewter. Seating is white embossed leather with a matching black leather floor.

Fine dining is provided with an English restaurant featuring a huge open fire, crystal studded Chesterfield seating, textured leather and 24 carat gold leaf walls and polished antique oak flooring. The nearby Thai restaurant has embossed velvet walls, four huge crystal chandeliers hanging from the vaulted ceiling, leather tables and banquette seating.

WENDY – THE ABERPORTH EXPRESS

"Beached" Edwardian rail carriage on Heritage Coast

WENDY ❽
THE ABERPORTH EXPRESS
Aberporth, West Wales

UNDER THE THATCH
Bryn Hawen
Henllan
Llandysul
Ceredigion SA44 5UA
0844 5005 101
post@underthethatch.co.uk
www.underthethatch.co.uk

ROOMS AND RATES
Low season (May) two-
night breaks from £252.
Seven nights in peak
season (August) at £657.
Pembrokeshire is only a 25
minute drive, however there
is no vehicular access to the
property itself. Access from
the car park is via a 300
yard level gravel footpath.
Prices include hot water,
electricity, heating and
the first basket of wood/
coal for the fire/stove.

This former Great Western Railway sleeping carriage has been relocated alongside a footpath in Wales with panoramic views of the Ceredigion Heritage Coast. Called Wendy after the character in Peter Pan, which was published the year before the carriage was built in 1905, it travelled the length and breadth of the Great Western line between England and Wales until it was retired in 1937.

Permission to build a permanent structure in this location would never be granted, so the opportunity to stay in something with its own history while you enjoy the view is particularly pleasing.

There are two insulated and oak-lined double bedrooms with proper sprung mattresses and a single children's bed, allowing you to sleep in comfort all year round. A modern kitchen and bathroom complete the rental package.

There is a lounge and dining compartment with a period 1930s dining table. Every room has uninterrupted country and/or sea views with open fields to the rear, and sea to the front. This is a peaceful location with no roads within 300 yards, and no neighbours or noise pollution.

The location is idyllic and your needs are catered for by a village pub, shop and food within a 5 minute walk – which includes a Chinese take-away and beachside café if you can't bear to cook.

VISITOR COMMENTS
• *Wendy is fantastic – What a location!*
• *Every day we walked to a different beach.*
• *A BRILLIANT holiday – weather great, views spectacular, dolphins & seals seen. Lots to explore lovely beaches, and great food ... we'll be back!*

GOTHIC TEMPLE

Temple folly in the manicured landscape gardens of Stowe

GOTHIC TEMPLE ❾
Stowe, Buckinghamshire

THE LANDMARK TRUST
Shottesbrooke
Maidenhead
Berkshire SL6 3SW
01628 825925
bookings@landmarktrust.org.uk
www.landmarktrust.org.uk

ROOMS AND RATES
The temple can accommodate
up to four guests in two
double bedrooms. Prices
for the whole property are
from £481 for a four-night
midweek break in January
to £1,826 for a week in
July/August. Disabled
access is limited because
of the spiral staircase.

Stowe School offered The Landmark Trust a long lease on this property in 1970, whose efforts provide income to maintain this splendid example of Gothic style architecture. Built in 1741, it is one of the last additions to the garden at Stowe formed for Lord Cobham. That same year, "Capability" Brown arrived as gardener, to begin his transformation of the landscape to create one of the finest landscape gardens in the world.

Lord Cobham decided to dedicate his new temple, designed by James Gibbs, "to the Liberty of our Ancestors", for which the Gothic style was deemed appropriate. Triangular in plan, with castellated gables, accommodation and facilities are contained in the three pentagonal turrets with large Gothic windows, decorated with knobbly pinnacles. The rooms are all circular inside, with mounded

LOCATION
Between Oxford and
Northampton, Stowe's
nearest major town is
Buckingham – which has all
the trappings of a successful
market town with shops,
pubs and restaurants.

stone pilasters and plaster vaults. The main vault of the central space is gorgeously painted with heraldry and from the first floor gallery you can start to appreciate the architectural majesty of the building. At the top of the staircase is a belvedere with stone seats offering a fine view of the landscape, now presided over by The National Trust.

The ground floor provides a kitchen in the base of one tower, and modern bath and conveniences in the second – if in rather surprising places. In between is a lounge with a view of the vaulted ceiling. Climbing the stairs encased in the third tower, you reach two double bedrooms – one in each tower, providing accommodation for four.

As might be expected in such a cavernous property, with high vaulted ceilings and solid stone walls, the effect of the heating system is slight – if any. Be prepared to wrap up well for early or late season breaks, or better still, ignore the temperature and just enjoy the amazing surroundings.

APPLETON WATER TOWER

Victorian water tower on Royal estate

APPLETON WATER TOWER ❿
Sandringham, Norfolk

THE LANDMARK TRUST
Shottesbrooke
Maidenhead
Berkshire SL6 3SW
01628 825925
bookings@landmarktrust.org.uk
www.landmarktrust.org.uk

ROOMS AND RATES
The tower sleeps up to four
people in two double rooms.
Prices for the whole
property are from £435
for a four-night midweek
break in January to £1,826
for a week in July/August.
There is a steep staircase
so it is unsuitable for
disabled guests or toddlers
without close supervision.

A public-spirited local landowner offered the lease of this exceptional Victorian tower to The Landmark Trust which, recognizing that there is seldom an opportunity to preserve a functional building like this, let alone one of such quality, mounted a successful appeal.

Designed by Robert Rawlinson, the foundation stone was laid in July 1877 by the Princess of Wales. The ground and first floors were the dwelling for the custodian, with a viewing room above reached by an outside stairway. In typically ingenious Victorian fashion, the flues from all the fireplaces passed through the centre of the iron tank to prevent the water from freezing – original, simple and practical.

The terrace on top of the tank is protected by an ornate cast-iron railing, and as from the room below, there is a view on all sides over miles of wide, open landscape. Here, on this exposed hilltop, you can even see a distant gleam of The Wash.

TO DO

Apart from marvelling at a view normally seen by birds, balloonists and pilots, the estate is an area of great wildlife diversity. The north Norfolk Broads are within reach, as are shingle and sandy beaches. In winter, it can appear bleak – however a crackling fire and a good pub are a time-honoured and satisfactory local remedy.

VISITOR COMMENTS

• *The view from the top of the tower is marvellous and you can see for miles over fields and cottages.*
• *I can vouch for the magnificence of the stars seen from the roof.*
• *Squeals of excitement as we explored the tower.*

CLEY WINDMILL

Historic windmill

CLEY WINDMILL ⑪
CLEY-NEXT-THE-SEA
Holt
Norfolk NR25 7RP
01263 740209
info@cleywindmill.co.uk
www.cleywindmill.co.uk

ROOMS AND RATES

The ground floor includes a circular sitting room where antique furniture and sofas nestle comfortably around a roaring open fire. The beamed dining room, part of the original warehouse built in 1713, has a warm and friendly atmosphere in which to dine. The upstairs rooms and galleries have stunning views over the marshes and the sea. In great demand as a wedding venue and for house parties, sleeping up to twenty in nine rooms on a B&B basis, it books a long time in advance. You are recommended to plan well ahead, especially for summer weeks – and as much as two years for weddings. Two night stays are required for all but winter midweek breaks. Prices per room are from £129 - £139 for a single midweek night and between £328 - £378 for a min 2 night weekend stay on a B&B basis in the mill.

LOCATION

The windmill stands on the north side of the village within walking distance of the excellent shops. It has uninterrupted views over the sea, the salt marshes and Cley Bird Sanctuary, with Blakeney Harbour in the distance. The large walled garden abuts the River Glaven, surrounded by reeds and tranquility.

Cley Windmill dates from the 1700s, although the tower was not completed until some time later. It is a well-known North Norfolk coastal landmark in a historically prosperous area that was a major East Anglian port for wool and grain. The windmill commands breathtaking views over the salt marshes to Blakeney Point and the sea, while nestling comfortably by the old quay alongside the flint-walled cottages of the village.

It has been accepting guests since around 1921 when it was first converted into a holiday home.

With improvements and renovations over the years, the original mill, old stables and boathouses have been converted into stylish bedrooms or self-catering retreats for independent holidaymakers.

The windmill provides a guesthouse of immense character, charm and comfort and is a fantastic experience to savour.

FRESTON TOWER

Lookout tower of unknown function

FRESTON TOWER 🕐
Near Ipswich, Suffolk

THE LANDMARK TRUST
Shottesbrooke
Maidenhead
Berkshire SL6 3SW
01628 825925
bookings@landmarktrust.org.uk
www.landmarktrust.org.uk

ROOMS AND RATES
A twin and double bedroom
on the third and fourth floors
provide accommodation
for up to four.
Prices for the whole
property are from £381
for a four-night midweek
break in January to £1,412
for a week in July/August.

LOCATION
On the banks of the River
Orwell outside Ipswich,
facilities are few, but walking
opportunities along the river
and towards Pin Mill abound.

No one really knows who built Freston Tower or indeed why it was constructed. The enigma of its existence points most closely to a wealthy Ipswich merchant called Thomas Gooding, who bought the land of Freston Manor in 1553. Further records have yet to be unearthed and archive notes of the area are few. Its crisp brickwork and distinctive blue diapering suggest that it was always intended to be an eye-catching landmark – perhaps as a lookout tower for Gooding's ships, or simply as an extravagant folly – making it one of the first recorded examples. It may even have been built with royal favour in mind, to coincide with Queen Elizabeth I's progress to Ipswich in 1561.

Set in an old and undulating parkland of oaks, sweet chestnut, cedar and beech trees, the architecture and construction is certainly exquisite. There are no fewer than twenty-six windows dotted over its six storeys, arranged in careful hierarchy. Intricate brick mullions and imitation-stone window surrounds no doubt tested the craftsmen of the day – as they have done more recently for its renovation.

The kitchen is on the first floor, with bathroom above. The next two storeys are bedrooms, a twin with double above, sleeping four in total. The sitting room then tops the tower on the fifth floor, to take advantage of unrivalled views of the River Orwell and its handsome modern bridge.

VISITOR COMMENTS
We have enjoyed living vertically for a week – sad to be coming back down to earth.

THE BALANCING BARN

Cantilevered silver barn looking over a nature reserve

THE BALANCING BARN ⑬
Living Architecture LLP
930 High Road
London, N12 9RT, UK
No phone
admin@living-architecture.co.uk
www.living-architecture.co.uk

ROOMS AND RATES
Vacation rental sleeping up to eight (four rooms) A low season midweek is from £759, high season full week £3068

LOCATION
The Balancing Barn is 5 km (3 miles) from the ancient village of Walberswick on the Suffolk Heritage Coast, just off the main A12 and 10 minutes from the quaint seaside town of Southwold.

Located on a site on the edge of a Suffolk Wildlife Trust reserve, this stunning property overlooks a small lake. Although the barn is clad in reflective steel tiles, it is unobtrusively located at the end of a tree-lined driveway set back from a quiet country road. It isn't until you view the property from the side that you appreciate that while half of the 30 metre long building is anchored to the ground, the other half juts out into the valley, with nothing but space underneath. This cantilevered construction balances the building on a concrete plinth embedded into the hillside, so although balanced, it feels solid underfoot. It looks amazing.

The property is filled with practical and usable features, showing the care and attention of the Dutch design team who crafted this construction. Stylish continental lighting illuminates each of the four double, en suite, bedrooms, kitchen/diner at the anchored end, and suspended over the valley – lounge area with fireplace. All along the sides of the barn are full-height windows and in the lounge area, a glass floor. This floor deserves special mention, as it overlooks the childrens' (and adults') swing that is suspended underneath the barn.

MARTELLO TOWER

Napoleonic coastal fortification

MARTELLO TOWER 14
Aldeburgh, Suffolk

THE LANDMARK TRUST
Shottesbrooke
Maidenhead
Berkshire SL6 3SW
01628 825925
bookings@landmarktrust.org.uk
www.landmarktrust.org.uk

ROOMS AND RATES
Accommodation for up to
four people in two rooms.
Prices for the complete
property are from £452 for a
four-night midweek break in
January to £1,842 for a week
in July/August. Cooking is
on an electric hob. There is
a solid-fuel stove for extra
heating in the sitting room.

LOCATION
Standing at the foot of the
Orford Ness peninsula,
between the River Alde and
the sea, the tower is only
a few hundred yards from
Aldeburgh. Many visitors
bring sailing dinghies.

This is the largest and most northerly of the chain of fortified towers put up by the Board of Ordnance to keep out Napoleon. Built in the shape of a quatrefoil to house four heavy guns, nearly a million bricks were used in its construction. Although they successfully deterred the French from invasion, in this exposed position the elements still attack. The installation of a purpose-made canopy over the main living space now provides significant protection with an agreeable nautical resonance of sails and canvas, however you should be prepared, during the rougher seas of winter, to expect that sometimes water will find its way inside. Sensitively restored by The Landmark Trust after it was purchased in 1971, both exterior brickwork and the vaulted interior are maintained to the typical high standards of the Trust.

Choose your companions wisely as the bedrooms are not fully divided, although they are screened from the central living area. Lying in bed, the echoes from the oiled teak floors provide a sense of being in a larger loftier space – yet you will hear your fellow guests as the acoustics are impressive.

THE HOUSE IN THE CLOUDS

Former water tank, in Merrie England village

SYLVIA LE COMBER ⑮
4 Hinde House
14 Hinde Street
London W1U 3BG
0207 224 3615
houseintheclouds@
btopenworld.com
www.houseintheclouds.co.uk

ROOMS AND RATES

With five bedrooms, there is space to easily accommodate ten people in a variety of double and twin rooms. Weekly lets are preferred and the minimum stay is two nights. A week in low winter season is around £2,130, rising to £3,200 in midsummer and for Christmas/New Year, inclusive of all taxes, towels, linen and utilities.

LOCATION

For arrivals by train the nearest station is Saxmundham, 5 miles away, served from London Liverpool Street, changing at Ipswich.

The House in the Clouds was originally intended to provide an adequate storage capacity for a basic water supply for Thorpeness village in 1923. Faced with the difficult task of hiding a rather hideous structure, the engineering team brilliantly disguised it as a house, which from miles around seems to be a cottage lodged 70 ft up in the trees. The supporting steel structure was boarded in to provide unique living accommodation, although for many years the accommodation did not include the very top of the tower, which housed the 50,000 gallon water tank. In 1977 the use of the tank for storage was discontinued and it passed into private ownership. As befits a structure that once held near 350 tons of water, the house is very sturdily built. The many tiny windows offer good light and ventilation. Last refurbished in 2002, it provides spacious accommodation for family holidays having five bedrooms, two with double beds, three with twin beds and an additional double sofa bed. Three bathrooms, drawing room, dining room and the magnificent "room at the top" give the finest views of Suffolk.

The five floors are connected by a total of sixty-seven stairs with four landings and five half-landings – resting seats for the less able on each landing. There is an iron spiral staircase on the fifth floor to the upper gallery.

THE MUSIC ROOM

More intricate Baroque plasterwork than you'll find in any museum

THE MUSIC ROOM ⑯
Sun Street, Lancaster

THE LANDMARK TRUST
Shottesbrooke
Maidenhead
Berkshire SL6 3SW
01628 825925
bookings@landmarktrust.org.uk
www.landmarktrust.org.uk

ROOMS AND RATES
Two bedrooms, sleeping four.
Prices for the whole property
are from £171 for a four-night
break in January to £647
for a week in July/August.

Squeezed into a little back alley behind The Sun hotel, this 1730s building was originally a summerhouse in the gardens of the hotel. Restoration was a huge undertaking, as access was near impossible and The Landmark Trust needed to buy the buildings on all sides and demolish them to give builders access to The Music Room itself. Such great efforts also necessitated the creation of a pedestrian square to preserve the striking façade and the glazing of the central Ionic arch to create a rather good ground-floor café.

Once you've climbed to the music room inside you suddenly appreciate what an exceptional property this is, as the Baroque plasterwork is hugely ornate and wouldn't be out of place in a royal palace. With a double bed in the main room, the walls are decorated with the muses: eloquence, history, music, astronomy, tragedy, rhetoric, dancing, comedy and amorous poetry; with Apollo over the fireplace. A fruitful goddess with a torch presides over the ceiling. One muse had vanished entirely and was recreated as a modern girl, big and busty, with a cheerful eye; she makes an excellent muse of dancing.

In the attic above, reached by a narrow stair, the Trust made a twin-roomed flat. From there and from the small terrace on its roof there are distant views over Lancaster (including a fine view of the castle from the sink!).

THE MACKINTOSH BUILDING

Charles Rennie Mackintosh designed property

THE MACKINTOSH BUILDING ⑰
Comrie, Perthshire

THE LANDMARK TRUST
Shottesbrooke
Maidenhead
Berkshire SL6 3SW
01628 825925
bookings@landmarktrust.org.uk
www.landmarktrust.org.uk

ROOMS AND RATES
Accommodation for up to
four, with nearby parking.
Prices for the whole
property are from £139
for a four-night midweek
break in January to £851
for a week in July/August.

LOCATION
Comrie is an unfussy
Highland town, with a
bridge over a pebbly river,
a whitewashed church
and a small square, on
the corner of which, right
at the centre of things,
stands this distinguished
and surprising building.

Designed by Charles Rennie Mackintosh, this building dates from 1903–4, when he was doing his very best work. It was commissioned by a local draper and ironmonger, Peter Macpherson, as a shop with a flat above and workrooms in the attics. The Landmark Trust was able to reunite the elements of the property in 1985, following purchase from the different proprietors, including original owner Mr Macpherson's granddaughter. The main room runs into the projecting turret, which gives it an airy feel, and a pleasant view of the River Earn and the wooded hills beyond. At the back is a long garden, reached by a passage from the street.

GUEST COMMENTS
• *It has made us quite determined to find out more about Charles Rennie Mackintosh.*
• *We were especially fond of the bay window— looking out on to the world of Comrie.*
• *The marriage of Mackintosh building to Landmark Trust is a truly happy one.*
• *A delightful flat, a charming and friendly village, magnificent countryside and enough to do and see to last a lifetime.*

THE PINEAPPLE

Stunning, elaborate, eccentric summerhouse

THE PINEAPPLE ⑱
Dunmore, Central Scotland

THE LANDMARK TRUST
Shottesbrooke
Maidenhead
Berkshire SL6 3SW
01628 825925
bookings@landmarktrust.org.uk
www.landmarktrust.org.uk

ROOMS AND RATES
There is a double and
twin room, as well as the
bathroom, in one wing of
the property. Walk outside
to access a lounge and
kitchen in the other wing.
Prices for the whole
property are from £227
for a four-night break in
January to £1,434 for a
week in July/August.

LOCATION
Between Falkirk and
Stirling, near Kincardine
bridge and Airth Castle.

The Pineapple is an elaborate summerhouse of two storeys, built for the 4th Earl of Dunmore. Though classical and orthodox at ground level, it grows slowly into something entirely vegetable; conventional architraves put out shoots and end as prickly leaves of stone. It is an eccentric work, of undoubted genius, built of the very finest masonry. It probably began as a one-storey pavilion, dated 1761, and only grew its fruity dome after 1777 when Lord Dunmore was brought back, forcibly, from serving as Governor of Virginia. There, sailors would put a pineapple on the gatepost to announce their return home. Lord Dunmore, who was fond of a joke, announced his return more prominently.

The Pineapple presides over an immense walled garden. This, in the Scottish tradition, was built some distance from the house to take advantage of a south-facing slope. To house the gardeners, stone bothies were built on either side of the Pineapple. These make plain, unassuming rooms to stay in, although you have to go outside to get from one part to the other.

The Pineapple and its surroundings are owned by the National Trust for Scotland. The Landmark Trust took on the lease in 1973 and restored all the buildings and the walled garden, now open to the public. At the back, where the ground level is higher, there is a private garden for guests, with steps leading into the elegant room inside the Pineapple itself.

WICKLOW HEAD LIGHTHOUSE

95 foot navigation beacon

WICKLOW HEAD LIGHTHOUSE ⑲
Dunbur Head, Co. Wicklow, Ireland

THE IRISH LANDMARK TRUST
25 Eustace Street
Temple Bar
Dublin 2
Ireland
+353 1 670 4733
bookings@
irishlandmark.com
www.irishlandmark.com

ROOMS AND RATES

Sleeping 4 in two double bedrooms, the complete property may be rented for a midweek break in January low season for €500. A full week in high season (July/August) is €1400 inclusive of electric central heating. Unfortunately, the property is unsuitable for guests who have difficulty with stairs as there are 109 steps to the kitchen on the top floor.

LOCATION

County Wicklow is just south of Dublin and in these rolling granite hills, lies the source of Dublin's River Liffey – used to make Guinness.

The octagonal stone tower known as Wicklow Head Lighthouse was originally one of a pair built in 1781 as a distinctive landmark to eliminate the confusion among mariners who wondered if they were at Howth or Hook Head. It is approximately 95 feet high, and still functions as a long established landmark for sailors.

The Lighthouse was originally lit by lanterns each containing twenty tallow candles. However, because they were high on the hill, and often obscured by fog, the towers were not effective and a new lighthouse was built lower down on Dunbur Head.

The original front tower has long disappeared from the landscape, and following a lightning strike to the rear tower in 1836, the lantern was destroyed. The interior was gutted on all floors, and it was decided that the cut stone shell of the tower should be preserved. A new roof was added and the present protective brick dome added in 1866.

The Irish Landmark Trust acquired the lighthouse in 1996, and set about conserving the tower. This involved replastering the internal and external walls, making and fitting 27 windows, wiring, plumbing, flooring and installing a water pumping system. When the stairs and timber floors were in place, 6 octagonal rooms were arranged vertically. Although the rooms are small, they have high arched windows set into walls which are almost a metre thick.

It is a peace seeker's haven with inspiring and refreshing views of the Irish Sea. The landscape and scenery surrounding the lighthouse provide a perfect backdrop for a unique and memorable break. The lighthouse is a truly inspiring place to stay.

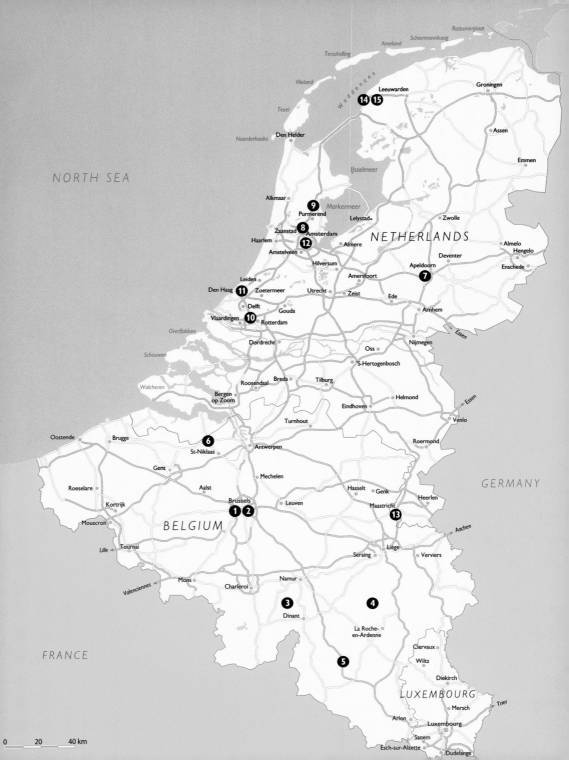

BELGIUM AND THE NETHERLANDS

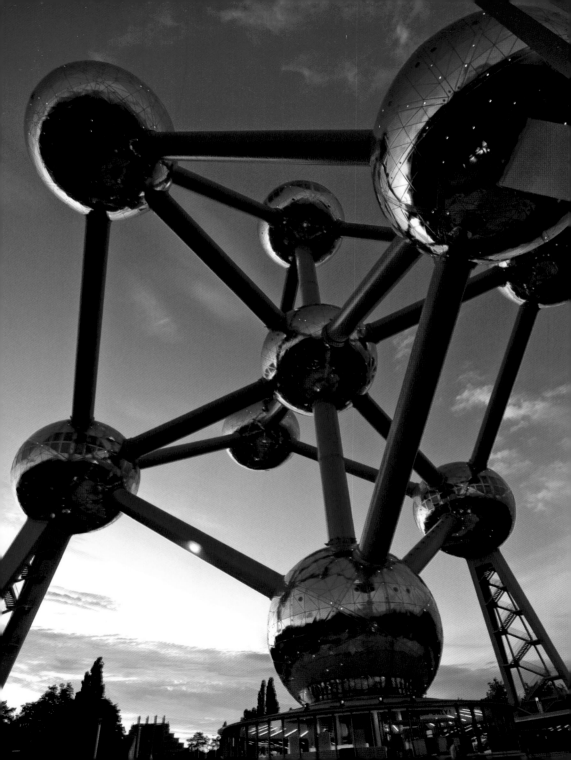

THE ATOMIUM

Primary-school group sleeping space inside The Atomium

The Atomium ❶
Atomium Square
1020 Brussels, Belgium
+32 493 03 44 02
julie.almau@atomium.be
www.atomium.be

Rooms and rates
One room sleeping
10 to 24 children.
All guests (children
and adults) pay €25 per
person to include:
use of facilities, night
caretaker, evening meal and
breakfast, guided visit.

Practical details
Children and accompanying
adults arrive at The Atomium
at 6pm. Generally a film is
shown, and all meals and
facilities are laid on in the
Sphere. Kids sleep in small
groups (three to four max) in
the mini-spheres. The next
morning, after breakfast in
the panoramic restaurant,
there is a presentation
about The Atomium. The
experience ends at 10am.
Capacity is between ten
(min) and twenty-four
(max) children, plus up to
two accompanying adults
on Monday, Tuesday and
Thursday – except on
Belgian public holidays.

The Atomium is a Brussels icon built for the 1958 World Fair Exposition, at a time when the belief in progress, science and modernity was immensely strong.

The structure symbolizes an iron crystal, magnified 165 billion times. Spanish artist Alicia Framis was commissioned in 2005 to create an educational project based on the building's characteristics and features, as well as its history and symbolic value.

The kids' sphere captures the optimism of a future enabled by technology and science, in a way that reflects the insights of the world in the twenty-first century.

One ball of The Atomium has been divided into separate functions: mini-spheres (water molecules) suspended from the ceiling to sleep in, the floor for workshops / playground, a "Petit Club Sandwich" and washing facilities. Children spend a night at The Atomium marvelling at the panoramic view of Brussels from its spheres.

PANTONE HOTEL™

Rooms themed by the Pantone colour chart

THE PANTONE HOTEL™ ❷
Place Loix 1
Brussels, B-1060, Belgium
+32 2 541 4898
info@pantonehotel.com
www.pantonehotel.com

ROOMS AND RATES
59 rooms and suites.
Room rates vary from
€69 to €250 (excluding
breakfast, which is €15
per day, per person).

LOCATION
The hotel is situated a
3 minute walk from
either Louise or Hotel des
Monnaies metro stations.

All colours used at the Pantone Hotel™ are referenced to the globally recognized Pantone Color Matching System® that allows standardized colour reproduction.

Designed by Michel Penneman and Oliver Hannaert, the hotel offers rooms with photography by esteemed Belgian photographer Victor Levy. From a design perspective, the hotel is built on an exceptional use of contrast; a white canvas provides clean space for saturated colours to pop. Both bright primary colours and warmer tones, displayed in photos, furnishings – even the chairs and coffee cups – add mood-shifting sparkle.

LA CLASSE

Back to school in style!

LA CLASSE ❸
1 Tienne Piot
Namur 5537, Belgium
+32 71 79 81 57
gite@laloux.be
www.laclasse.be

ROOMS AND RATES
Seven Rooms
Prices for the whole
property from €2100 for
the whole week. Weekend
and midweek options are
also available from €1900

LOCATION
Situated in the village of
Denée, which is part of
the commune of Anhée, La
Classe used to house both
the municipal offices and
the village school. It is in
the heart of the village, less
than 100 m from the village
square, on a one-way street
at the far end of the square.
Denée is in the heart of
one of the most beautiful
regions of Belgium, only 5
minutes from the Molignee
valley and the Abbey of
Maredsous, and the gardens
of Annevoie, close to Dinant
and Namur. A number of
great trips can be arranged,
including group tours on
Vespas and family treks on
a pedal-powered railcar.

Anne and Jean-Luc Laloux specialize in architectural photography, and travel the world in search of exceptional homes designed by the best contemporary architects. This enriching experience has inspired them to create beautifully appointed holiday accommodation which combines both the conviviality of group living with the aesthetic pleasure of great design.

La Classe (The Classroom) is exceptional and a long way from any school memories that you may have! The quality of the materials, the wonderful use of space, the selection of designer furniture, the highest standard of facilities and fittings — all the ingredients to create a special atmosphere are here: the rest is up to you.

LA BALADE DES GNOMES

Amazing fairytale rooms and a Trojan Horse suite

LA BALADE DES GNOMES ❹
Rowe de Remoleu 20
Heyd Nr Durbuy
6941, Belgium
+32 472 20 86 23
info@Labaladedesgnomes.be
www.labaladedesgnomes.be

ROOMS AND RATES
From €115 for the smallest
double rooms to €230 for the
Trojan horse for two people,
inclusive of breakfast.

LOCATION
15 minutes' drive from
Durbuy (10 km / 6.5 miles)
and 2 hours from Brussels.

These ten extraordinarily decorated and furnished bedrooms evoke ideas from the four corners of the world, reinterpreted as fairy tales.

Hidden in an unassuming farmhouse up a pleasant - but not particularly noteworthy - country lane, this amazing property was designed and built by architect and visionary hotelier Mr Noël. Originally opening an innovative restaurant, *La Gargouille* (The Gargoyle), specializing in delicious dishes using local ingredients and bio-organic produce, he has taken inspiration from fairytales to construct these amazing bedrooms, next door to the restaurant.

Defying normal classification, these rooms highlight incredible imagination, attention to detail and sheer audacity to delight guests.

EURO SPACE CENTER

Experience astronaut training – unique in Europe!

EURO SPACE CENTER ❺
Rue devant les Hêtres 1
Transinne 6890
Province of Luxembourg,
Belgium
+32 61 65 01 34
booking@eurospacecenter.be
www.eurospacecenter.be

ROOMS AND RATES
Twenty-four sleeping
rooms with six to nine
beds per room.
Courses are from two days
/ one night for a minimum
of twelve students from
€139 inclusive of activities,
dinner and breakfast.

LOCATION
Situated in the Belgian
Ardennes, about
90 minutes from Brussels
and 1 hour from Liege,
the centre is alongside
highway E411 – exit 24.

The Euro Space Center is a recreational and educational discovery centre about space, related science and technologies. Unique in Europe, it allows families to live as astronauts and to experiment astronaut training for a number of residential programmes targeting French, Dutch, English and German-speaking groups. Space camps are suitable for youngsters from the age of 8 within the scope of a school project or on holiday. Programmes include various workshops, simulation exercises, observations and lectures on space and its exploration.

The main goal here is to let young participants experience the training that has been set up for astronauts during fifty years of space exploration. Every year the ESC hosts groups from all around the world to stay and visit. About 100,000 youngsters aged between 10 and 16, from Belgium, Europe and elsewhere, have already taken part in the programmes. They gain their own experience in simulators, training machines, workshops, on courses of two to six days' duration.

As well as a full-size mock-up of the Space Shuttle and the European Space Agency's Columbus – a module of the International Space Station – a number of micro-gravity simulations and exercises are available.

VERBEKE FOUNDATION

Sleep in a giant intestine!!!

VERBEKE FOUNDATION ❻
Westakker
9190 KEMZEKE
(Stekene), Belgium
+32 37 89 22 07
info@verbekefoundation.com
www.verbekefoundation.com

ROOMS AND RATES
Single-bed apartment
and four tent rooms.
One night in CasAnus
costs €120 for two,
including breakfast.
Tent: €35 for two people.

LOCATION
The property is located
alongside the sliproad
running parallel with the
N49-E34 Antwerpen-Knokke
motorway, near exit 11.

In 2007, art collectors Carla and Geert Verbeke Lens opened an art sanctuary to showcase modern and contemporary art, bringing together young artists alongside more established names. Combining Culture, Nature and Ecology the site encompasses 12 ha (30 acres) of nature reserve and 20,000 sq m (215,000 sq ft) of indoor space. After an initial interest in abstract painting, the collections were reoriented to collages and assemblages of mainly Belgian artists. In recent years the collection was expanded to include contemporary art and bio-living art. The Verbeke Foundation has since become recognized as one of the largest private initiatives for contemporary art in Europe.

Artist Joep van Lieshout has created "CasAnus", an amazing polyester sculpture that represents a huge enlargement of the human digestive tract, so large indeed that you can rent the structure and sleep in it overnight. It offers twin beds, a table, shower and toilet. CasAnus is equipped with lights, water and electric heating.

Also available is Kevin van Braak's "Camping Flat" art installation, consisting of a 12 m (40 ft) high scaffold structure with tents on each of four floors. Each floor has an artificial grass flooring surface, a "campfire" and the whole structure is covered in fine netting to protect you from birds.

Our exhibition space will be no oasis. Our presentation is unfinished, moving, unpolished, contradictory, messy, complex, unharmonious, unmonumental and live – like the world outside the museum walls. Geert Verbeke

AIRPLANE SUITE

Fly to your dreams in this converted plane

Vliegtuigsuite ❼
De Zanden 61B
Teuge (near Apeldoorn)
7395 PA, The Netherlands
+31 6-19388603
info@hotelsuites.nl
www.hotelsuites.nl

Rooms and rates
One luxury suite
An overnight stay for
two, including a luxury
breakfast, costs €350.

Once the transport for top bosses of the German Democratic Republic government, this 1960 Ilyushin 18 has been converted to a single luxury suite for two. The plane is 40 m (130 ft) long and now comes equipped with a little more luxury than its former owners would have approved of – let alone publicly enjoyed!

With a jacuzzi, shower, infrared sauna, minibar, flat-screen TVs (three of them), Blu-ray DVD / entertainment combo (plus a selection of DVDs), and a pantry with coffee/tea-making facilities, you can enjoy a great deal of comfort – while still sleeping on a plane.

This plane flew dignitaries including Erich Honecker during its early life as transport for favoured politicians. Transferred to commercial airline use in 1964, it flew up to 120 passengers and four crew in slightly less comfort with East German airline, Interflug, until 1986. Destinations included Cuba, China and Vietnam as well as Soviet Russia. After German reunification the plane served as a restaurant for fifteen years until it was acquired in 2007 and converted to a hotel.

HOTEL INNTEL ZAANDAM

Madcap collection of classic Dutch building façades

INNTEL HOTELS AMSTERDAM ZAANDAM ❽
Provincialeweg102
1506 MD
Zaandam, The Netherlands
+31 75 631 1711
infozaandam@inntelhotels.nl
www.inntelhotels
amsterdamzaandam.nl

ROOMS AND RATES
160 rooms and suites.
From €95 per night in a
standard double room

LOCATION
Situated next to Zaandam
railway station on the direct
line to Amsterdam Central
station, about 12 minutes
away. Schiphol airport is only
16 minutes away by train and
you're directly connected to
the RAI Congress centre too.

One look at the twelve-storey Hotel Inntel Zaandam will astound you.

Like a collection of different houses, assembled on top and alongside each other in a life-size jigsaw, you'll simply be amazed – and undoubtedly amused.

Chief Architect Wilfried van Winden of WAM, the director of the Delft-based bureau, modestly suggests that he didn't set out to shock. Instead, his wish was to avoid the bland, impersonal approach of traditional hotels, and create something more like a home-from-home, with façades based on traditional Zaanstad houses: "From a stately notary's dwelling," he quotes, "to workers cottages."

Inside, rooms retain their personal feel, themed according to traditional elements of Zaandam's heritage and manufacturing past. The Zaanstad region has a long tradition of rich aromas and rooms are decorated with wall-sized enlargements of advertisements for Zaandam-manufactured chocolate, cheese, mustard and biscuits, as well as black and white photos from the bygone industrial past of the town.

CONTROVERSY TRAM HOTEL

Sleep in a tram or a train

CONTROVERSY TRAM HOTEL ❾
Konongspade 36,
1718 MP Hoogwoud
The Netherlands
+36 226 352693
info@controversy.nl
www.controversy.nl

ROOMS AND RATES

Five double rooms
The five rooms cost from
€60 per person per night,
including a great breakfast,
tour of the amazing Appel
home, tourist tax and
cleaning. If you plan to
stay for several nights, the
rate reduces on the second
night to €50 per person
per night and the third
night or more only €40
per person per night.

LOCATION

A local map will help you
find Hoogwoud, which is
off the main road between
Amsterdam and Harlingen.
Once you're within range,
it's easy to see Controversy
– there aren't many places
with trams, trains and fighter
planes in their garden. If
you're arriving by train and
planning to stay several
nights, ask Irma if she can
pick you up – or arrange a
taxi from the local station.

In a remote corner of The Netherlands, crazy and friendly owners Frank and Irma Appel have created themed tram bedrooms in either end of two city-centre tram railcars that used to run on the streets of Amsterdam and in Germany. They've also converted a railway carriage into a luxurious double room, complete with a jacuzzi in the shape of a giant Mexican sombrero. The trams have double beds, shower and toilet facilities. They are arranged into four themed compartments: Italian (smoking), French (smoking), English (non-smoking) or American (non-smoking). A library with books, comics and old videos is provided for tram and rail carriage guests to while away a lazy afternoon. Painted silver, it looks like a spaceship – but is actually the escape pod from an oil rig, floating on a mini lake all its own.

Next to the trams and railway carriage is the Appel house, "Controversy" – named after their love of the similarly titled Prince album. You can't help but appreciate the lifestyle that Frank and Irma have created. They sleep inside a London double-decker bus installed in the living room, their kitchen and breakfast area is a converted French van and their house is decorated with cars and motor paraphernalia. A Cadillac and an amazing trike made from a Mercedes car in your lounge? A Lamborghini next to your bedroom? It's all at the Appel house.

There isn't a full restaurant on site, but Irma provides a wide breakfast selection from the main house and is always on hand with helpful advice.

Outside in the grounds, a MiG fighter plane is perched on top of a road roller – providing a surreal landmark for the property to help it stand out from the surrounding flat land around Hoogwoud.

EUROMAST TV TOWER

Two luxury rooms on top of a TV tower

EUROMAST ⑩
Parkhaven 20
3016 GM Rotterdam
The Netherlands
+36 10 24 1 1 7 88
suites@euromast.nl
www.euromast.nl

ROOMS AND RATES
Two double suites
Both suites are €385.00
per night including an
extensive breakfast (in your
suite or at the brasserie at
the top of the tower).

LOCATION
Euromast is in the Parkhaven,
but consider the parking
restrictions if arriving by
private car, or otherwise
consider takinge a taxi. While
parking carnets are available
from the tower shop, it can
prove expensive if you leave
your car for the day, and
you'll need to perhaps feed
the meter again when you'd
rather be tucked up in bed
enjoying your breakfast.

The Euromast tower is a feature of the skyline of Rotterdam, and has been a regular tourist attraction since it was built in the 1960s. Already known as a great brunch venue, there are also two suites available for advance booking – "Heaven" and "Stars", perched 100 m (over 300 ft) above the city. After the crowds have gone, suite occupiers are left to the night skyline in luxury with polished wooden floors, comfortable double beds, minibar and room service through to 1 am. For night owls, reception is open 24 hours. With the amazing view below, the wireless internet is perhaps unnecessary, although mobile phone coverage is very poor (if not non-existent). The larger of the two suites, "Heaven", has a great view of the docks and can provide a child's cot (at additional charge). It also has a great shower and designer black toilet tissue. The smaller suite, "Stars", looks over the Rotterdam city skyline, and has a bathroom jacuzzi.

Balcony access is from 10 pm until 10 am, so you have plenty of time to enjoy the cool night air and really enjoy the view of city and docks far below. We were warned that in winter, the rooms can be a little cold (they have big windows, but are only single glazed), but more worrying perhaps is that not only are you able to look out – the occupants of the other suite can look in from the shared balcony … so consider closing the curtains if your nightwear isn't suitable for external viewing …

CAPSULE HOTEL

Escape overnight in your own survival pod

Capsule Hotel ⓫
Verheeskade 287, 2521DE,
Den Haag
The Netherlands
No tel. • denis@vlnr.info
www.capsulehotel.info

Rooms and rates
Two pods
The luxury package costs
€150 per capsule, while the
survival-plus and survival
offerings cost €100 and €70
respectively, inclusive of
taxes. Discounts for students.
All capsules can be booked
up to a month ahead and a
deposit of 10% is required to
confirm your reservation.

Based at F.A.S.T. (Free Architecture Surf Terrain) - a unique and artistic surfers village on the boulevard of Scheveningen near The Hague, your room is a bright orange survival pod which once saw service on an oil rig platform. Originally built in 1972, they are 4.25 m (14 ft) in diameter and unaltered apart from the addition of a lock on the outside and an "emergency" chemical toilet inside. While not everyone's luxury choice, each pod provides cosy protection from the elements for up to three occupants.

First created for accommodation as an art project in 2004, owner Denis Oudendijk has eight different models ready for use and is currently working on additional locations in central Amsterdam and Nantes, France.

A number of overnight packages are available from a basic survival package with a sleeping bag and emergency rations, through to a James Bond themed luxury offering. This package has to be tried (think of the final escape pod scene of From Russia with Love), for its kitsch factor of a disco mirror ball, fairy-light decorations and sleeping bags with silk liners replacing the basic cotton. To get you in the correct mood, the luxury package also includes a DVD player with all the Bond movies on disc. In addition, your survival box is transformed into a luxury version with goodies including sparkling wine and a collection of vodka bar miniatures to create your own Martinis, shaken or stirred!

Whatever your choice of package, the bathroom facilities are non-existent / basic, with baby-wipe towels and bottled water to replace traditional shower and toilet facilities.

THE LLOYD HOTEL'S SEVEN-PERSON BEDS

With your family, your friends, or whoever you like!

LLOYD HOTEL **12**
Oostelijke Handelskade 34
1019 BN Amsterdam,
The Netherlands
+31 20 561 3607
Fax: +31 20 561 3600
post@lloydhotel.com

ROOMS AND RATES
From €90 for their one star
accommodation in a room
with bathroom down the hall
to €250 for their 5 star suites

Located just outside the city centre in the Eastern Docklands neighbourhood, which was built in 1875, the Lloyd Hotel occupies a building that was constructed in the 1920s to house immigrants. In the 1940s, it was converted into a prison and remained so until 1989, when the City of Amsterdam took over the site to rent it out to artists. The building took on its current role as a hotel in 2004.

Based on an original concept, the hotel offers rooms with comforts and services varying from one-star to five-star.

In the five-star range, the hotel has two particularly unique rooms, each with a bed that can sleep up to eight people – the perfect choice for large families or for groups looking to have a little fun.

There's a nice cafeteria-style restaurant with a designer atmosphere on the ground floor.

KRUISHERENHOTEL

Sleep in a 15th-century monastery

KRUISHERENHOTEL
MAASTRICHT 🔟
Kruisherengang 19-23
NL 6211 NW Maastricht
The Netherlands
+31 43 329 20 20
info@kruisherenhotel.com
www.chateauhotels.nl

ROOMS AND RATES
Fifty rooms and suites
in former cloisters.
Fifty of the sixty rooms are
in the cloisters, with the
others in the gatekeeper's
lodge or new building. We
recommend confirming
which you require when
booking. From €199 per
person per night, based
on a couple sharing.

LOCATION
The hotel is in the centre
of Maastricht, on the restored
Kommelplein square,
about 5 minutes' walk
from the more famous
Vrijthof square.

Serving originally as a monastery and church for the Order of Kruisheren (Crutched Friar) since 1438, this building fell into disrepair in the 1980s. The transformation into a luxurious, contemporary designer hotel was undertaken by Camille Oostwegel, who commenced large-scale renovation in late 2000. The character of the original monastery has been maintained in this complex project as, although designer furnishings and modern amenities have been provided in the rooms, they contrast with the stained-glass windows, Gothic vaulted ceilings and elegant stonework of the original building. Antiquity and modern design have been interwoven throughout. A mezzanine area has been created in the former nave of the church to provide a breakfast area with views of the town through the large windows of the former chancel. The nave also houses reception and the hotel lobby, plus a wine bar for "spiritual" refreshment. Side chapels are converted to lounge areas and the spacious stone corridors give a feeling of quiet reflection.

The bedrooms are housed in the former cloisters behind traditional solid oak doors that block unwanted noise from any guests unaware of how well sound travels along these stone corridors. Comfortably furnished, the rooms have wooden floors and quality designer fittings. Wall hangings, photographs and paintings tell stories of legends such as that of Saint Gertrude, patron saint of travellers, and it's obvious that a lot of thought has gone into the restoration to retain the "monastery mood".

HARLINGEN LIGHTHOUSE

Sleep overlooking the town in this lighthouse tower

HARLINGEN LIGHTHOUSE ⓮
Havenweg 1
Harlingen Lighthouse,
The Netherlands
+36 517 414410
www.vuurtoren-
harlingen.nl

ROOMS AND RATES
One double suite. The double room costs €319 for a couple sharing for 2011/12 including tax. Breakfast is included in the price, delivered to the bottom of the lighthouse steps by the friendly hostess team. The team doesn't accept online reservations as they prefer to assist you by phone. Reception is mainly open in the morning, but first check their website for any additional questions.

LOCATION
The lighthouse is next to the Harlingen Dokkade (docks) station, close to the city centre of Harlingen, only 10 minutes' walk from the shops and restaurants of this thriving Dutch seaside town.

First built: 1920–1922, Architect: C. Jelsma Restored: 1998–1999, Architect: B. Pietersma Position: 53 10' 09" NL; 05 25' 04" EL Highest lookout point: 24 m (80 ft) above average floodwater

Sister property to the Dockside Crane hotel, Harlingen Lighthouse is not difficult to find – it's in the heart of the historic docks, towering above the surrounding houses. Look for an Art Deco beacon. Unlike many lighthouses it has no need to be remote, as it protected navigation from the sandbanks around the port itself. After climbing the eighty or so steps, you uncover a three-storey luxury haven, providing all-round panoramic views from your bedroom and upstairs lookout, with added facilities including TV, tuner/CD unit, minibar and a hot-drinks facility. The bedroom is beautifully equipped, not surprisingly with a hand-made (and comfortable) bed. One floor below the bedroom is the bathroom with a giant shower and facilities. Thankfully, the designers have ensured that the nautical theme is retained and the original lantern room at the top provides a VHF radio so you can hear the movements of shipping traffic, as well as wind speed and direction meters. The outside balcony can also be accessed, should you wish to brave the elements yourself. Looking down on the city and docks below is endlessly fascinating – and looking down on the birds flying even more so. Binoculars are provided!

Inside is surprisingly spacious, however some of the steps and ladders are steep – so pack your belongings in a soft bag, and travel light.

Harlingen Lighthouse formed part of a network of lights along the Dutch coast. Eighteen of the twenty lighthouses are still in use. The other disused lighthouse, in the Hook of Holland, is now a museum.

DOCKSIDE CRANE

Rotate your private industrial crane

DOCKSIDE CRANE ⑮
Dokkade 5
Harlingen,
The Netherlands
+36 517 414410
www.vuurtoren-
harlingen.nl

ROOMS AND RATES

One double suite. The double room costs €319 for a couple sharing for 2011/12 including tax. Breakfast is included in the price, delivered unseen into your room by the magic column lift. As with the other Harlingen entries, the team doesn't accept online reservations. Reception is mainly open in the morning, but first check their website for any additional questions first.

LOCATION

Close to the city centre of Harlingen, you're only a 10 minute walk from the shops and restaurants of this thriving Dutch seaside town, and about 2 minutes from the Dokkade railway station. Harlingen is a working dockside town, but you're in the quiet historic port, next to the harbour-master's office and historic square -rigger boats.

The second of three unusual hotels in Harlingen, this amazing converted dockside crane has been the recipient of intelligent engineering and dedicated devotion rarely seen in a private home – let alone in a hotel property. Replacing the old external ladders with modern lifts to gain entry, the old machine room in the body of the crane has been transformed into a luxurious bedroom that wouldn't be out of place in the most modern of designer hotels.

Managers Willem and Carla have kept the existing observation windows and industrial feel, but have added comfort, warmth and the latest flat screen and audio equipment to create a fantastic environment to enjoy a childhood dream for many – your own personal, WORKING crane. Even though they've fitted a luxury double shower and designer toilet, the crane can still swirl around controlled from the comfort of the driver's cabin. A fantastic breakfast of fresh local pastries, eggs and a deli selection is included, delivered magically via the internal lift to your bedroom. Entry to the crane itself is effortless as lifts are provided to the main bedroom area. The top picnic area and crane cabin are accessed via a ladder from the main bedroom, but you rarely feel enclosed or uncomfortable about the height. This is a solid, trustworthy block of metal, and even when rotating you recognize that it's capable of lifting tons of goods, so you and your bedroom don't pose a problem.

Arrive promptly, and take advantage of the panorama, as rain or shine this is a spectacular vantage point from which to view the old docks. With a crane at your disposal, you're sure to find yourself spinning the platform instead of watching the DVDs supplied.

Following booking acceptance and payment, the Harlingen crane team will send you a comprehensive arrival pack. Even though the lifts allow entry for even the most vertigo-challenged and fitness-free, pack your belongings in a soft-sided bag, as one of the lifts is small and will only accept a small bag and you at the same time.

FRANCE

UN LIT AU PRÉ®

"Where overworked city dwellers live like Robinson Crusoe."

UN LIT AU PRÉ® ❶
Côte de Nacre (Calvados),
Pays d'Auge (Calvados),
Baie du Mont-Saint-
Michel (Manche),
Portes du Perche
(Orne), Vallée des
Evoissons (Picardy),
Plateau de Millevaches
(Haute-Vienne)
and Auvergne (Allier).
Other farms welcome
"Un Lit au Pré®" every year
Contact: Guillaume Wibaux
Tel. 01 41 31 08 00
www.unlitaupre.fr
info@unlitaupre.fr

ROOMS AND RATES
6-person tents
(maximum 5 adults)
Weekend (Friday 4pm
to Monday 10.30am):
from 295€ to 415€
depending on the season
Easter weekend: 435€
Pentecost weekend: 475€
Weekend of the Ascension
(5 nights): 575€
Mid-week: Monday to
Friday: from 235€ to 515€
Full week: Friday to
Friday: from 414€ to 835€
depending on the season
Open from Easter to
All Saints' Day

Guillaume Wibaux is a passionate man. His numerous travels, constant contact with locals, love of beautiful scenery, and desire to get back to the basics, even for a few days, encouraged him to adopt a concept that is highly popular in England and the Netherlands. That was how "Un Lit au Pré®" (A Bed in the Meadow) was born in 2008.

This carefully designed concept allows a family (up to 6 people) to share a farmer's life while remaining independent and spending a few days in a beautiful and comfortable tent. These 45m² tents, which are all identical, were designed especially for "Un Lit au Pré®". They include a living-room, a "guest-room" with bunk beds, a master bedroom, and an incredible box-bed large enough to hold 1 or 2 children. The front part of the tent can open up to create an outdoor living space.

A woodstove, the showpiece of the tent, stands in the centre of the living-room. It serves to heat the tent, but also for cooking. Here, you'll find no television, computer or electricity, just the sounds of nature – those of the animals and farmers.

With help from the farmers, the children take part in feeding and milking the animals, and, if they're lucky, they'll witness an animal birth. The farms are chosen in a very selective manner in favour of farmers who have a strong desire to share their lifestyle and who show true generosity. Each farm has a storeroom where the family can find food staples: products from the farm or neighbouring farms. Here, the owners don't provide a prepared breakfast, but you'll find fresh milk, eggs, and bread baked fresh in an on-site bread oven. On the farm, the children are treated like kings: bike-rides, games of hide-and-seek in the hay, or a nightly stroll to admire the stars after an evening spent playing games or reading by candlelight.

LA GARE DES ANNÉES FOLLES
(THE ROARING TWENTIES TRAIN STATION)

The only PLM train car in France turned into a hotel

LA GARE DES ANNÉES FOLLES ❷
77, rue de la Gare
62840 Sailly-sur-la-Lys
Tel. 03 21 02 68 20
www.lagaredesanneesfolles.fr
chefdegare@
lagaredesanneesfolles.fr

ROOMS AND RATES
7 compartments, 2 showers
and 2 lavatories, parlour,
garden and terrace
1-person compartment: 41€
2-person compartment
(bunk beds): 51€
2 one-person compartments
with connecting door: 71€
Nuptial suite
(double bed): 91€
Breakfast: 6.50€
To reserve
the entire car: 370€
Restaurant open daily,
closed Sunday evenings
and Mondays
Open year round

There are only 2 PLM train cars remaining in France: one is at the railway museum in Mulhouse, and the other near the former Bac Saint-Maur railway station. It is in this old 1930 train car, with its original mahogany and sycamore woodwork with mother-of-pearl accents, that 7 guest-rooms were professionally installed and renovated. Only the showers are new.

Acquired by the SNCF (French national railway company) in 1938, this sleeping-car, along with 12 others that once made up the train, was pulled by a steam engine and connected Paris to Lyon and the Mediterranean, making for a very luxurious overnight trip.

Today, the compartments can accommodate 1 or 2 people on bunk-beds; the former restaurant area at the end of the car has been transformed into a nuptial suite with a double bed.

Breakfast is served in the adjacent railway station which, thanks to its luggage racks and bottle-green-coloured seat cushions, has retained its original ambience. The décor of the waiting area and restaurant has been entirely redone in Art Deco style: pearl chandeliers, unmatched porcelain dishes, an old clock and antique books.

Truly a trip back in time.

PARC CANOPÉE (CANOPY PARK)

Sleep in a hammock hung in the treetops

PARC CANOPÉE ❸
Benoît Sautillet
Forêt de Chatel
5, rue Quillette
02290 Ambleny
Tel. 06 10 47 53 02
www.canopeeaventure.com
Ben.sautillet@orange.fr

ROOMS AND RATES
28 hammocks, including
one 2-person hammock
25€ per person and
35€ per person for
the "Plum'arbres"®
Minimum age requirement
for the hammocks
is 6 to 8 years old
Open Saturday evenings
in April, May, June and
September, and every night
in July and August

After its Accrobranche (tree-climbing) courses and bungee-jumping activities, which are offered both day and night, Parc Canopée (Canopy Park) decided to expand its business and offer overnight accommodation in hammocks or "Plum'arbres"® (hanging tents, see page 122) hung in pine trees at heights varying from 3m to 15m.

You reach the hammocks by ladder or, in a more athletic manner, by following a tree-climbing course. Then there's the difficult exercise of getting into the hammock, which, of course, quickly begins to rock.

Afterwards, you'll be given your pillow and sleeping-bag, and perhaps a book and flashlight. Finally, it's time for lights out and you're left to spend a night under the stars surrounded by the sounds of the forest and still attached to your harness in order to keep you from falling.

If the weather turns bad, don't worry. A supervisor will come quickly to lead everyone to shelter under a tent.

In the morning, breakfast is served in the forest.

LE CHÊNE PERCHÉ

To get back to nature, get high!

LE CHÊNE PERCHÉ ❹
Domaine de la Vénerie
08460 Signy l'Abbaye
Tel. 03 24 53 35 62
or 06 37 32 49 65
www.lecheneperche.com
infos@lecheneperche.com

ROOMS AND RATES
4 tree-houses accommodating
2 to 8 people
85€–110€ per night
for 2 people,
depending on the tree-house
105€–115€ for 3 people
125€–135€ for 4 people
210€ for 8 people
Breakfast included,
served at the base of the tree
Bring your own sleeping-bag
Special prices for the treetop
activity courses (3 children's
courses with another for
children 6 years or younger
to open soon, 4 adult courses,
5 Tyrolean traverse courses)
Bike rental: mountain bikes,
hybrid bikes, tandem bikes,
and child bike trailers
Open April to November

It took 3 years for a team of passionate people to bring this park in the middle of Signy forest at the heart of the Ardennes region to life, with its treetop climbing courses and tree-houses offering overnight accommodation. The tree-houses are located either at the edge or at the heart of the forest, and they all offer a unique panorama of the valley and forest. You reach them by climbing a ladder and then taking a footbridge. Although specialized equipment isn't required, it would be best to avoid wearing high heels.

The Lisière and Sous-bois tree-houses (13m and 8m above ground respectively) can accommodate children 6 years or older. The Canopée tree-house, one of the highest in France, stands at a height of 16m and can accommodate children 14 years or older; one must climb 2 ladders and take a suspended footbridge to get to the top of the oaks.

Lastly, a final tree-house can accommodate up to 8 people, with no minimum age requirement, and is thus perfect for large families looking to gain some height (it has 3 levels ranging from 3m to 8m above ground).

None of the tree-houses has running water or electricity, but they do have eco-friendly toilets.

The park offers other activities, including mountain and tandem biking, pedagogical hikes for children, and various nature-related demonstrations to learn more about the forest.

CHEZ BERTRAND

Spend the night in a refurbished 2CV car!

CHEZ BERTRAND ❺
93400 Saint Ouen
Tel. 06 63 19 19 87
www.chezbertrand.com
bonjourbertrand@gmail.com

ROOMS AND RATES
4 apartments
The Loft:
from 250€ for 2 nights
for 1 to 3 people,
to 700€ for 7 nights
for 5 people.
The Studio:
from 230€ for 2 nights
for 1 to 3 people,
to 500€ for 7 nights.
"L'Appart":
from 230€ for 2 nights
for 1 to 3 people,
to 630€ for 7 nights
for 4 to 5 people

Located just a few steps away from Saint Ouen's famous flea market, this former fireplace store was sold in 2006 to Bertrand, who kept the original façade but entirely renovated the interior into a 40m² loft, a duplex, a studio apartment, and his own apartment.

In the "garage"-style loft, an actual red 2CV convertible has been turned into an astonishing bed. Guests can even watch a movie (200 TV channels) on a large flat-screen TV "drive-in" style. A round bed lies behind the car.

Entirely covered in aluminum foil, the Studio is a veritable masterpiece: each sheet was crumpled, and then glued, before finally being protected with varnish. As for the shower, it was installed in a rain water tank.

In a nearby street at the heart of the flea market, the owner also refurbished "L'Appart" (The Flat): a very "love" red-and-white entryway, a rather girly pink bedroom (pink window film and pink walls), a living-room with green walls and a sofa bed, and a small orange kitchen with a disco ball. Children will love the Haribo boy whose body is filled with candy.

MUSEUMOTEL L'UTOPIE

A one-of-a-kind place

Museumotel l'Utopie ❻
Île Haüsermann
88110 Raon l'Étape
Tel. 03 29 50 48 81
www.museumotel.com
museumotel@orange.fr

ROOMS AND RATES
9 bubble-bungalows
for 1 to 5 people
55€ to 100€
for 1 person
70€ to 160€ for 2 people
Additional person: 10€
Breakfast: 7€
Various packages
including champagne
and breakfast are available

The utopian and visionary architect Pascal Haüsermann built this extravagant, even outrageous, place in 1967 and 1968 on a site surrounded by two branches of a river. The first motel, which operated from 1968 to 1998, remained closed for 4 years before being bought and reopened in 2007. The original "pop" theme was kept, but all modern amenities were added.

The site is now a motel, an eco-museum and a place for artistic expression. You can spend the night, have a drink at the Utopia café (serving Breizh cola, poppy -or violet-flavoured drinks, and more), visit an art exhibit, attend a concert, or simply stroll through the garden among the contemporary sculptures.

The bubble-bungalows, which respect all the styles from the 1950s to the 1970s and are furnished with period designer furniture (Charles Eames, Verner Panton), are each decorated in a unique and personalized manner. They each have a shower, sink and toilet.

Among the different bungalows, there's the "Love Bubble" with its heart-shaped double bed, and the orange "69" bubble whose psychedelic plastic décor will delight fans of the 1970s.

LA FERME AVENTURE (ADVENTURE FARM)

Spend the night in a plane, a glass pyramid, or on a bed of straw in a hayloft

LA FERME AVENTURE ❼
15, Côte de Hardémont
88240 La Chapelle aux Bois
Tel. 03 29 30 11 79
www.nuitsinsolites.com
lfaventure@free.fr

ROOMS AND RATES
Tree-house
(2 to 5 people):
100€ per night
Caravelle (2 to 6 people):
110€ per night (25€ heating
charge November to March)
Pyramid:
100€ per night
Yurt (2 to 5 people):
100€ per night
4 tipis,
2 small tipis for children
(2 to 10 people):
65€ per night
4 hayloft rooms
(2 to 10 people):
65€ per night
16€ per additional guest
Open April to October

On the property of Denis Duchêne and his son Benoît, the options for spending an unusual night are quite numerous: you can sleep in a tree-house, a yurt or a tipi, or, if you're looking for something even more original, you can sleep in a glass pyramid or a real Caravelle airplane. Construction of the Caravelle, the flagship of French aviation, began in 1955; 282 were built. Baptized Ohrid (after a lake on the border of Albany and Macedonia), the Caravelle 233 that Denis bought had 20,000 registered flight hours and had taken its last flight in the colours of the Corsair airline before being dismantled and transported to the Vosges mountains. Today, it has been transformed into a loft, with a living-room, bedrooms, barbecue grill, and a 3000m² enclosed lawn.

For those who dream of sleeping under the stars, but in warmth and sheltered from wild animals, the glass pyramid offers a truly unique experience. There are no curtains on the windows, but the pyramid is far enough away from the other buildings to ensure your privacy.

A final experience is to spend the night in a hayloft on a bed of straw.

LE CARRÉ ROUGE (RED SQUARE)

Sleep in a red cube with no running water or electricity

LE CARRÉ ROUGE ❽
Route de Santenoge
52160 Villars-Santenoge
Haute-Marne, southern part
of the Langres plateau
Tel. 06 62 03 98 38
www.leconsortium.
com/carrerg
jf.guenin@free.fr

ROOMS AND RATES
130€ for the weekend
plus 30€ per extra day
(e.g. 190€ for 4 days)
1 to 6 people (maximum
occupancy: 6 people)
Sheets, comforters,
blankets, pillows, towels,
dishes, wood for cooking
and heating, as well as
gas lamps are provided

DIRECTIONS
From Paris by car,
on the A5, take exit
Langres-sud. On the A6,
take the exit Auxerre-sud,
then Chablis, Tonnere,
Châtillon-sur-Seine, and
Recey-sur-Ource. At Recey,
take the road to Langres.
At Villars-Santenoge,
follow the road to Chaugey.
At the old wash house,
turn right on the road
to the Chalmandrier Farm
(ferme Chalmandrier).

A masterpiece of contemporary art by Gloria Friedmann, the Carré Rouge (Red Square) is a cube with a south-facing side painted red and a north-facing side made entirely of glass. Lost in the middle of the French countryside on the Langres plateau, the site is superb – the perfect place for a unique, romantic getaway or a family vacation.

The cube has two levels: the lower level holds the kitchen and dining space, while the upper level houses three double beds.

Without running water or electricity, staying in the cube is a return to a more primitive state that will delight children. Rainwater is collected by a water pump, and potable water is available at the village fountains, just a short walk away (700m). For lighting, oil lamps and candles are available, as is the woodstove (no need to cut the wood, it's graciously provided!) which serves for both cooking and heating, thanks to a central pipe that diffuses the heat throughout the cube.

Jean-François Guénin, the manager, runs an equestrian centre just a short distance from the cube. Guests can thus go horse riding through the surrounding forests and hills.

SALINE ROYALE (ROYAL SALTWORKS)

Spend the night in an exceptional historic monument

SALINE ROYALE ❾
25610 Arc et Senans
Tel. 03 81 54 45 00
www.salineroyale.com
colloques@salineroyale.com

Built on the order of Louis XV, the Saline Royale (Royal Saltworks) of Arc and Senans is the masterpiece of Claude-Nicolas Ledoux. Classified as a world heritage site by UNESCO, this monument was built from 1775 to 1779 to recuperate salt from low-content salt water.

After the end of this industrial activity in 1895, the 11 buildings were saved from destruction many times, and, now restored, they are the site of cultural activities, seminars, colloquiums and artist studios. Although the Saltworks is not actually a hotel, it is possible to stay there.

Twelve comfortable rooms restored by architect Wilmotte (others will soon be available) welcome guests in a sharp, clean style. The architect even designed the furniture, which was then manufactured by the Saline Royale engineering department with wood from the nearby

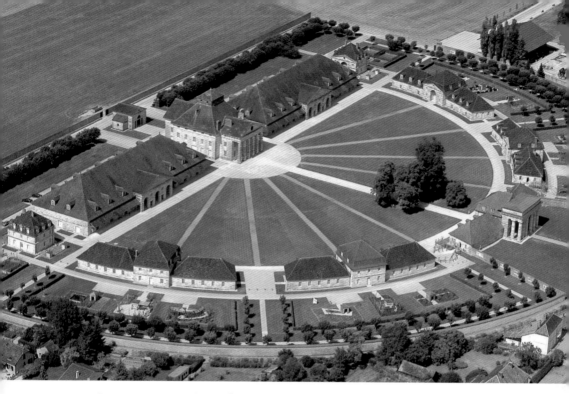

ROOMS AND RATES
12 rooms: 70€ to 82€
for 2 people,
depending on the room
and the season,
includes entrance
to the Saltworks
(site and museums)
Buffet breakfast: 10€

Chaux forest, the second largest natural forest in France. In fact, it was partly due to this forest that the Saltworks was built here. In addition to the northern winds which, by simple evaporation, gave the brine a much higher salt concentration before being heated, the abundant quantity of wood was an essential element in the production of salt: it was used to heat, evaporate and transform the brine.

It is when the tourists have left that guests truly realize what a privilege it is to spend the night at this historic site.

The diversity of the Saltworks' activities means guests can meet conference participants in suits, performers rehearsing (Jane Birkin was recently sighted here) or gardeners working for the Garden Festival held every year from June to October.

> It was through the œil-de-boeuf window in the central building, which housed the director's office, that the latter kept watch over the Saltworks.

LA FERTÉ ABBEY DOVECOTE

A beautiful dovecote at the heart of an abbey

LA FERTÉ ABBEY DOVECOTE ❿
Mr. and Mrs.
Jacques Thénard
La Ferté sur Grosne
71240 Saint Ambreuil
Tel. 03 85 44 17 96
www.abbayeferte.com
abbayedelaferte@aol.com

ROOMS AND RATES
Dovecote: 2-room suite
with a bathroom:
from 77€ for 2 people
to 119€ for 4 people
Open May to September
Gatehouse:
from 97€ for 2 people
to 129€ for 4 people
Open Easter to mid-October

La Ferté Abbey is a classified historic monument from the 18th century. It was the first abbey to be founded by Saint Bernard in 1113, and was one of the largest Cistercian abbeys in France.

Although the church disappeared after the French Revolution, the ancestors of the current owners, who bought the site, preserved the superb 70m-long abbey residence. The monks' magnificent former refectory has been converted into a reception hall.

The abbey also possesses a rather exceptional dovecote: it still has the cells where the birds nested, which is rare nowadays. A beautiful bathroom has been installed, and, on the mezzanine level, you'll find a bedroom with a double bed.

The gatehouse at the entrance to the abbey was the home of the monk gatekeeper, who was in charge of monitoring visitors. It has also been charmingly restored and turned into guest-rooms.

The English-style park that surrounds the abbey invites guests to take a pleasurable stroll.

It is also possible to visit the entire domain in the company of the owner.

LE JARDIN DE LA LICORNE
(THE UNICORN'S GARDEN)

Spend the night in a 1950s British bus

LE JARDIN DE LA LICORNE ⑪
14130 Les Authieux-
sur-Calonne
Tel. 06 87 06 69 01
www.gite-roulotte-
deauville-honfleur.com
jardin-de-la-licorne@
wanadoo.fr

ROOMS AND RATES
1 British bus for 4/5 people
1 caravan for 4 people
3 caravans for 2/3 people
Rented as self-catering
cottages (no breakfast)
Sheets and towels
are provided
Bus: 100€ per night
or 190€ for the weekend
Caravans: 90€ per night
or 160€ for the weekend
Open mid-February
to mid-November (heated)

Antoine has installed some very charming caravans in his garden (the oldest is 110 years old). With his circus caravans or movie caravan dating from the 70s, he was one of the pioneers of this trend in France (see the many other caravans in France offering overnight accommodation), but, in a more original manner, he has also outfitted an astonishing British bus.

The bus, which is rather impressively carpeted in a red Scottish motif, is equipped with 2 double beds, a vintage bar with original seats, a shower and a kitchenette.

The site is stunning and pleasant, just 7km from Pont-l'Évêque and 18km from Deauville.

The property also includes a sculpture studio that is open on Saturday afternoon.

DOMAINE DE LA COUR AU GRIP

"Spending the night in a barrel? Simply intoxicating."

DOMAINE DE LA COUR AU GRIP ⑫
Mr and Mrs Esnard
14340 Repentigny
Tel. 02 31 63 85 85
or 06 72 78 53 72
lacouraugrip.blog.capital.fr
paulette.esnard@wanadoo.fr

ROOMS AND RATES
90€ for 2 people,
gourmet breakfast included
Reduced rates for stays
of 3 nights or more
Table d'hôte dinner:
25€, includes cocktail,
appetizer and a half-bottle
of cider (regional specialties
made with cider or
international cuisine)

At the heart of Normandy's Cider Route, just a few kilometres from Beuvron-en-Auge (which is listed among the most beautiful villages in France), lies the 19th-century cider-making property of Paulette and Patrick, with its beautiful half-timbered house that is so typical of the region.

The estate possesses several buildings reminiscent of its origins: cheese dairy, sheep barn, stable, cider houses, distillery, and, most importantly, a cider press, from which Paulette and Patrick salvaged cider barrels. Whereas some of them served to decorate the kitchen or were turned into furniture, Patrick took one and turned it into a cabin for his children. Then they added a table and chairs, and it became a place to enjoy a cocktail or dinner.

And then one day they wondered why they couldn't sleep there, too, which is why guests can now spend the night in a 10,000-litre barrel.

Don't miss Paulette's table d'hôte dinners and culinary classes (she once taught in a catering school).

CHÂTEAU DE CANON

Europe's highest tree-house

Château de Canon ⓲
14720 Mézidon-Canon
Tel. 02 50 67 10 74
or 06 15 41 85 90
www.coupdecanon.fr
coupdecanon@gmail.com

Rooms and rates
4 tree-houses
120€ to 190€ per night,
breakfast and complimentary
cocktail included
Dinner: 25€
Open year round
Heating provided in winter

Three spectacular tree-houses have been built in the park of the beautiful 18th-century château of Canon.

The Laizon tree-house stands 10m above ground, and the Cascade tree-house, at 16m above ground, was the highest in France at the time of its construction, but it's the château of Canon's third tree-house that is the highest in Europe, at 22m above ground.

It is smaller than the others, but it offers the same charm and comfort, which means it's of very high quality.

In the morning, guests hoist their own breakfast up to the tree-house: hot drinks, croissants, chocolate croissants, and organic apple juice.

It is also possible to order an evening meal, prepared by a caterer, that you can enjoy in your tree-house in the romantic glow of candlelight or an oil lamp.

THE CHÂTEAU DU VAL D'ARGUENON'S TREE HOUSES

Tree-houses in exceptional trees

THE CHÂTEAU DU VAL D'ARGUENON'S TREE HOUSES 🔴
Notre-Dame de Guildo
22380 Saint-Cast-le-Guildo
Tel. 02 96 41 07 03
www.chateauduval.com
chateau@chateauduval.com

ROOMS AND RATES
3 two-person tree-houses
from 120€ to 130€ per night,
breakfast included
(delivered at 9am at
the base of the tree)
Bring a fully charged
mobile phone
Tennis court

If magical and enchanted places exist, then the Château du Val d'Arguenon is one of them. Owned by the same family for centuries (the château was sold once, but was bought back a few years later by a relative), it is now home to a large, welcoming family whose members each participate in welcoming guests or taking care of the magnificent 50-acre grounds that are home to a large number of palm trees.

The property occupies a unique location. A narrow drive at the bend of the road from Notre-Dame de Guildo to Saint-Cast-le-Guildo leads to the château. Park your car behind the château, then walk around to admire the view of the sound and small beaches waiting to welcome you. The ever-changing light is a magnificent spectacle that you can continue to admire from your treetop bedroom or tree-house terrace.

The property's beautiful trees are home to 3 tree-houses. The distance between them leaves guests with the feeling that they are alone in the world, which lets them fully appreciate this little corner of heaven.

PLUM'ARBRES®

A tent hanging from a tree

PLUM'ARBRES® **15**
Á un fil
Tremargat (22)
Belle Ile (56)
Other sites welcome
Plum'Arbres® tents each year
Tel. 06 85 63 63 67
or 02 96 36 58 87
www.a-un-fil.com
info@a-un-fil.com

ROOMS AND RATES
Nights at heights
of 2m or less:
40€ per night for 2 people
Nights at heights
of more than 2m:
80€ per night for 2 people
Tent capacity: 2 adults
and 1 or 2 young children
(reduced rates for children)
Breakfast: 4.50€
(in partnership with
local businesses)
Meal: 12€ to 18€
Bring your own
sleeping-bag,
flashlight and fully
charged mobile phone.
Stays are cancelled
during thunderstorms
or strong winds.
Open May to September

Specialized in hanging furniture, the "Á un fil" company has recently begun offering a new way to sleep in the trees. Since tree-houses have become a classic among the "unusual" ways to spend the night, they had to find something more inventive and extreme. That is how hanging camping was born.

The concept is simple – guests spend the night in a tent hung from a tree.

With a floor made out of catamaran netting and customized mattresses, some guests have claimed that they slept better here than in their own home!

The highest tents hang about 12m above ground. The less brave can choose to sleep at a much lower height, which makes it easier to get in and out of the tent.

GUEST COMMENTS

"It has a pleasant rocking motion, and it's soft, warm and comfortable."

LOUËT ISLAND

Treat yourself to an island, without spending a fortune

LOUËT ISLAND ⑯
29660 Carantec
Tel. 02 98 67 00 43
www.carantec-tourisme.com
info@carantec-tourisme.com

ROOMS AND RATES
Capacity: 10 people
(8 in the house,
and 2 in the labourer's
workhouse)
188€ for 1 day and 1 night
(or 18.40€ per person
for a group of 10)
251€ for 2 days and 2 nights
(maximum length of stay)
Open from April to
October (no heating)
Transport to island available
on demand by contacting
Carantec Nautisme
(Carantec Water Sports)
Bring a mobile phone,
sheets, pillowcases
and sleeping-bags

Louët Island is located in Morlaix Bay, 350m off the coast of Carantec. On a breathtaking site opposite the Château du Taureau, a rocky peak is home to the island's famous white lighthouse, which is featured in numerous books about Brittany. The lighthouse was inaugurated on 31 December 1860, and later automated in the 1960s. In 1998, the Lighthouse and Beacon administration placed it in under the management of the village of Carantec, which decided to open it up to the public.

Note that guests sleep in the lighthouse-keeper's quarters, not at the top of the lighthouse.

KASTELL DINN

The lifestyle of fishermen in the 19th century

KASTELL DINN ⓱
Hameau de Kerlouantec
29160 Crozon
Tel. 02 98 27 26 40
www.gite-rando-bretagne.com
info@gite-rando-bretagne.com

ROOMS AND RATES
Quille en l'air:
75€ for 2 people
Caloge:
100€ for 2 people
Breakfast included
Open year round

Kastell Dinn is a 17th-century longhouse that is typical of the half-rural, half-maritime settlements along the Cap de la Chèvre (Goat's Cape). It is located at the end of a dead end road in the tiny village of Kerlouantec, just 2km from the beach and the town of Morgat. The main house has 5 bedrooms, but others can be found in the garden, where the owners have created living quarters in two boat hulls that were going to be destroyed.

Anchored in the region for many years (Patricia bears the name of a hamlet on Cap de la Chèvre), the owners have thus brought back to life a fisherman's tradition. The géomoniers (seaweed fishermen) sometimes used old boat hulls that could no longer be used on the water to build less costly lodgings.

The result is stunning and gave life to the "Quillle en l'air" (keel up) room, also called the "lover's room", a small stone house whose roof is an upside-down boat hull.

The "Caloge", on the other hand, is a thatched-roof house built in a boat hull.

Other houses with boat-hull roofs, called the "Quilles en l'air", can be found in La Falaise Municipal Campgrounds in Equihen, in the Pas de Calais region. Rue Charles Cazin – 62224 Equihen Plage.
Tel. 03 21 31 22 61. www.camping-equihen-plage.fr, camping.equihen.plage@orange.fr, 8 keels (2 people, 4 people, 5 people). Rates: 55€ to 95€ per night for 2 people depending on the season. Reduced rates for stays of 3 nights or longer: 270€ to 540€ per week for 2 people, depending in the season (400€ to 690€ for 5 people). Open from 1 April to 31 October.

THE LIGHTHOUSE OF KERBEL

The only lighthouse in France where guests sleep at the top

THE LIGHTHOUSE OF KERBEL **18**
71, route de Port-Louis
56670 Riantec
Tel. 06 08 21 37 74
www.pharedekerbel.com
contact@pharedekerbel.com

ROOMS AND RATES
From April to September,
the entire property
is to let (lighthouse, cottage,
outbuilding, heated pool
and sauna) by week:
2000€ to 2650€ per week
From October to March:
lighthouse rental 550€
(Saturday 10am to Sunday
5pm; or Tuesday 10am
to Wednesday 5pm)
Valentine's Day: 700€
New Year's Day: 700€
Additional night: 100€

It was while reading the auction notices in the Ouest-France newspaper that Daniel became curious to visit the Kerbel lighthouse. When he arrived at the top, he fell in love with the view and decided to buy it.

Contrary to most traditional lighthouses, here guests don't sleep below in the lighthouse-keeper's quarters, but at a height of 25m after climbing 123 stairs. The 360° view of Groix, Lorient and Quiberon Bay, through the large bay windows, is extraordinary.

The charming keeper's house can accommodate 6 people, and Daniel has installed a sauna in the former fire tower, which has been cut and lowered.

LA VILLA CHEMINÉE (CHIMNEY VILLA)

A house set on a giant 15-metre high chimney!

LA VILLA CHEMINÉE ❶⓽
44260 Bouée
Reservations : 06 64 20 31 09
www.uncoinchezsoi.net
contact@uncoinchezsoi.net

ROOMS AND RATES
from 95€ to 99€ per
night for 1 or 2 people
Open year round

DIRECTIONS
by Cordemais

La Villa Cheminée (Chimney Villa) is an extraordinary artistic project designed by Japanese artist Tatzu Nishi for the Estuaire 2009 Nantes-Saint-Nazaire art event. This work of art eventually became permanent and it is now possible to spend the night in it. The artist installed a typical 1970s villa at the top of what clearly resembles a factory smokestack (he took his inspiration from the château de Fer, the largest fossil fuel power plant in France).

Located at the head of Ile de la Nation, the villa has an unrestricted view of the Loire estuary and the rocky Sillon de Bretagne.

The house has a well-equipped kitchen and bathroom on the bottom floor, and a bedroom with a double bed on the upper floor.

A stunning little garden surrounds the house.

"Un coin chez soi" also offers other original places to stay in Rennes, Nantes and Larmor-Plage.

LA VILLA HAMSTER

A giant hamster cage

LA VILLA HAMSTER [20]
Un coin chez soi
2, rue Malherbe
44000 Nantes
Reservations : 06 64 20 31 09
www.uncoinchezsoi.net
contact@uncoinchezsoi.net

ROOMS AND RATES
109€ for one night,
180€ for 2 nights.
High-speed Internet

Yann Falquerho likes to surprise people. In the smallest house in the city centre of Nantes, a former 18th-century caretaker's house, he decided to design a room in a giant hamster-cage to allow guests to slip into the skin of these little creatures.

A real steel wheel 2m in diameter, identical to that of this little rodent, allows guests to take a morning jog after having spent the night 2.5m above the floor. A metal ladder leads to the bed-cage, where you have to crawl on all fours, just like a hamster entering a tunnel. The wheel can be transformed into a table or a couch.

Yann Falquerho has pushed his idea almost to the limit: he has designed a metal and wood cube which activates a hydraulic system that lets guests quench their thirst, and a feeding dish filled with seeds – they're edible and organic. You'll even find hamster hoods so you can live the experience to the fullest!

> "Un coin chez soi" also offers other original apartments, such as "the underwater cabin of Captain Nemo", Jules Verne's famous hero. Here, guests sleep on a waterbed while listening to sounds of the deep sea. Metal passageways add to the impression of being in a submarine.

L'AMARANTE

A night for two on a boat

L'AMARANTE ㉑
1 bis, rue des Perrières
37500 Candes-Saint-
Martin (between
Chinon and Saumur)
Tel. 02 47 95 80 85
www.bateauamarante.com
info@bateauamarante.com

ROOMS AND RATES
300€ for 2 people,
all-inclusive (cruise, buffet
dinner and breakfast)

Sometimes called "coches d'eau" (horse-drawn barges) in reference to travellers in the 18th and 19th centuries (in contrast to "coches à terre" or stagecoaches which carried numerous travelers and merchandise), the superb traditional boats L'Amarante and La Belle Adèle now welcome visitors. Although the former can accommodate up to 34 people for a cruise, and the latter up to 26, L'Amarante can accommodate only 2 overnight guests.

Traditionally, the boat casts off at the end of the day for a wonderful one-and-a-half-hour cruise. Viewed from the water, the Saint-Martin Collegiate Church and, later, the château de Montsoreau are impressive indeed. After dinner, the boat berths for the night at the joining of the Vienne and Loire Rivers, and the crew slips away, leaving the lucky couple alone on board. The next morning, the captain delivers breakfast.

Note that there's no shower on board!

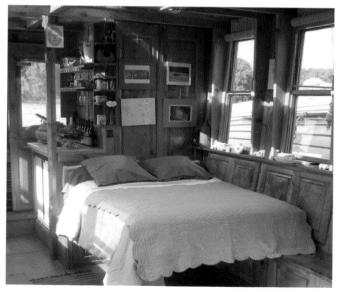

THE BURON OF NIERCOMBE

A timeless refuge

THE BURON OF NIERCOMBE ❷❷
15800 Saint-Jacques-des-Blats
Tel. 06 80 24 23 33
www.niercombe.fr
contact@niercombe.fr

ROOMS AND RATES
Capacity: 4 people
(and 2 people in the annex)
3-day weekend (2 nights)
minimum: 950€
(350€ for each
additional night)
The rate includes transport
to the buron in a 4x4,
and a kitchen stocked with
enough food for 2 dinners,
a lunch and 2 breakfasts.
Open May to October

The Buron of Niercombe is a former cheese dairy, at an altitude of 1450m, that you reach by taking a 4x4 on a private drive, accompanied by a mountain guide who will come to pick you up on the day of your departure. In the meantime, you'll be able to enjoy the solitude and the countryside's wild beauty – an exceptional experience. The buron is a traditional stone building with a lauze stone roof that is found in mountain pastures. Traditionally in the Auvergne region, the stockbreeders in the valley who own the pastures use them in the summer months. The burons are used to house the cheese-making equipment and to lodge the cheese-makers. Many burons have been abandoned, but some are now being used again, like that of Niercombe. The interior décor is simple, but welcoming. The furniture and flooring are made of wood, and there is a stairway leading down to the kitchen and bathroom below the main room. The water comes from the property's own springs. The Buron of Niercombe, which was built on a ledge more than 300 years ago, overlooks the Cère valley. It provided shelter to shepherds up to the 1940s, but was then left abandoned to the nature of the Monts du Cantal for over 60 years. It took 4 years of restoration work to turn it into this enchanting, timeless place.

Other burons where you can dine or spend the night
The Buron de la Thuillière (or Tuillère) in the village of Thiézac (tel. 04 71 47 06 60), access by car by taking the Curebourse Pass above Vic-sur-Cère. 15 beds in a stable. Meals.
The beautiful **Buron de la Fumade Vieille** (contact Bernard Montimart: 06 71 77 09 04 or 04 71 47 13 64. fvbc@orange.fr). Awarded 3 ears of corn by Gîtes de France. Open April to October.
Buron de la Combe de la Saure, in the village of Brezons. To reserve a table: 04 71 23 04 34. Regional dishes (+/−16€). No lodging.

LES DEUX ABBESSES

A village where each house is a bedroom

LES DEUX ABBESSES ㉓
Le Château
43300 Saint-Arcons-d'Allier
Tel. 04 71 74 03 08
www.lesdeuxabbesses.com
abbesses@relaischateau.com

ROOMS AND RATES
14 rooms
Half-board per day
per person for 2 people,
includes a room for 2,
afternoon tea, dinner,
breakfast, and water from
the mini-bar: 210€ to 340€
Open from Easter to
All Saints Day

The village of Saint-Arcons-d'Allier, located at the start of the Haut-Allier gorges, in the Haute-Loire region, was brought out of oblivion a few years ago thanks to the efforts of a mayor who accepted a hotel project in the hopes of seeing his village live again.

Perched 540m above sea level, the village, which possesses a 12th-century castle adjoining a small Roman church, had been deserted by its inhabitants up to the 1980s.

Today, the Deux Abbesses Hotel (named after Isabeau and Gabrielle Lafayette, whose cloister occupied a part of the castle in the 16th century), fills both the château, where you'll find the reception desk, lounges and the restaurant, and several houses throughout the village.

The entire village was renovated in such a way that you can still imagine what life used to be like here: the alleys connecting the various rooms were rebuilt in the traditional style, and some of the houses have been left untouched.

The room with a canopy bed made from birch tree trunks is a highly prized room, as is the lovely terrace garden offering a view of the valley that allows guests to relax while remaining hidden from view.

GUEST COMMENTS
"Spending a single weekend in this magical place allowed me to recharge my batteries."

L'ÎLE AUX OISEAUX

A suite in a "tchanquée" cabin

L'ÎLE AUX OISEAUX **24**
Les Sources de Caudalie
Chemin de Smith Haut-Lafitte
33650 Bordeaux-Martillac
Tel. 05 57 83 83 83
www.sources-caudalie.com
reservations@sources-caudalie.com

ROOMS AND RATES
650€
Breakfast: 24€

Located at the heart of Bordeaux's vineyards, the Sources de Caudalie Hotel possesses an extraordinary suite, called the "Île aux Oiseaux" (Bird Island), the name of an island in Arcachon Bay where one can find "tchanquée" cabins (beach houses on wood poles).

A pontoon leads to the house built entirely of wood and on piles. On the lake, your only neighbours will be the swans — perfect for a romantic night away from it all.

The cabin has recently been fully redecorated by Maison Martin Margiela who has conceived an avant-garde atmosphere (a blend of white, grey and black, with touches of red and trompe l'oeil effects) that is in total contrast to the cabin's exterior.

LES ECONOMIES D'ENEGIE A L'ERE DU RECYCLAGE

Théorie : "Rien ne se perd, rien ne se crée, tout se transforme" Lavoisier

Applications possibles :

- Si j'étais anorexique, je n'aurais pas à payer ma facture d'EDF
- Si je devenais un être à sang froid, je pourrais chauffer mon appartement à 35°C
- Si je ne buvais pas d'alcool, ma voiture pourrait consommer plus et donc rouler plus vite
- Si je ne respirais pas, mes plantes d'appartement seraient plus vertes
- Si j'étais inactive, je pourrais accélérer la vitesse de calcul de mon ordinateur
- Si je ne me lavais pas, l'eau du robinet serait buvable
- Si je ne parlais pas, la radio pourrait fonctionner sans pile
- Si je dormais sans rêver, je ne paierais pas la redevance télé

LE JARDIN D'HÉLYS-ŒUVRE

A real work-of-art estate

LE JARDIN D'HÉLYS-ŒUVRE 25
Domaine des Gissoux
Route départementale 705
24160 Saint-Médard-
d'Excideuil
Tel. 05 53 52 78 78
Free entry year round,
daily, 3pm to 7pm
or by appointment
http://lejardindhelys-oeuvre.fr
jardin.d.helys@wanadoo.fr

ROOMS AND RATES
6 double rooms,
50€ to 60€ per night
Breakfast: 5€
Self-catering accommodation:
320€ to 500€ per week
depending on the season
French "chèques
vacances" accepted
Open year round

In 1995, Alain Piot di Massimo (the father), Moniqa Ray-Bool (the mother), Claude Piot and Lorenzo (the sons) bought the Gissous estate, a 19th-century mansion, and invited artists to express themselves freely on a 32-acre area of the grounds.

The result is frankly stunning. From *in situ* creations to temporary works, the site itself has practically become a work of art.

Today, the mansion welcomes artists and visitors interested in adopting a work of art – the room where they'll stay – for a night, or two, or more.

LE PIC DU MIDI

*"There is no one who was born under an unlucky star.
There are just people who don't know how to read the stars."*

LE PIC DU MIDI ㉖
65200 La Mongie
Tel. 0825 00 2877, Monday
to Friday (office hours)
www.picdumidi.com

Since the summer of 2006, it has been possible to spend the night at the summit of the famous Pic du Midi and live a truly extraordinary experience.

Although the rooms are purposefully rather sparse so as to accentuate the incredible human adventure of the Pic du Midi (the rooms are those normally used by researchers), they all have an unrestricted view of the Pyrenees, which, in addition to the site's unique ambience, more than compensates for any eventual discomfort.

After arriving by cable-car in the late afternoon (before 5pm–6pm from June to September), guests visit the site and then enjoy a cocktail while watching the grandiose spectacle of the sunset, at 2877m above sea level. Next comes dinner (regional specialties) before the long-awaited

observation of the stars and night sky. A professional guide is present to lead guests up to the Charvin dome which is equipped with a 400mm telescope. In the morning, after watching the sun rise over the Pyrenees, guests can visit the domes in the scientists' quarters, the only time when they are open to the public.

Don't forget to bring very warm clothes (ski cap, gloves, good shoes, fleece jacket, windbreaker) so you can participate in the outdoor activities under good conditions. At this height, it can turn cold quickly, regardless of the season.

The summit of the Pic du Midi became a site for observation and scientific study at the beginning of the 18th century. Construction of the observatory began in the 1870s and was completed in 1882. The first cable-car was installed in 1952. Although the government considered closing the observatory in 1994, the Midi-Pyrenees region took action and renovated the site.

BELREPAYRE AIRSTREAM

A true change of scenery

BELREPAYRE AIRSTREAM ㉗
09500 Mirepoix
Tel. 05 61 68 11 99
www.airstreameurope.com
info@airstreameurope.com

ROOMS AND RATES
9 trailers
110€ to 200€ per night,
for 2 to 4 people
depending on the season
Reduced rates for stays
of 3 nights or longer
Can be rented by the week
Possible to rent a parking
space if you have
your own trailer or camper
more than 30 years old
Sheet and towel rental
Jacuzzi, massages
Open from the end of April
to the end of September,
by reservation only

With its magnificent view of the Pyrenees, the hillside campsite of Perry and Coline, the charming proprietors of the Belrepayre farm, has become the European capital for the owners of Airstream trailers.

There wouldn't have been such a revival of these trailers, the most elegant form of transportation in the USA from 1950 to 1970, if it weren't for Perry, a restoration expert. Kept in perfect condition, these trailers are in high demand by those looking for an original, retro experience or by film crews.

If you're a disco fan, don't miss the Apollo lounge, the bar of one of the restored Airstream trailers, which becomes the main attraction in the summer, when Perry organizes movie nights and shows. With a little luck, he'll be behind the turntables with his superb collection of 1950s–1970s vinyl records and his son, Coréo, will do a few magic tricks.

The Airstream trailers are fully equipped for cooking. They each have an awning or parasol, a barbecue grill, an outdoor table and chairs, and deckchairs. In the camp, you'll also find a little stand where you can buy staple goods: fresh bread, croissants and ecological specialties from nearby farms. The camp also has ping-pong tables and a football table.

Guests can also enjoy a red ciderwood whirlpool bath or a massage in the Mongolian yurt.

L'APPART DES ANGES

A barge full of charm, on the Canal du Midi

L'Appart des Anges 28
Péniche "Les Anges d'Eux"
Canal du Midi
34420 Cers
Tel. 04 67 26 05 57
or 06 11 11 05 87
www.appartdesanges.com
contact@appartdesanges.com

Rooms and rates
3 rooms
128€ to 155€ per night
for 2 people,
depending on the season
and length of stay,
brunch included
2-night minimum rental;
weekly rental
in July and August
Gourmet basket:
55€ for 2 people,
everything from
the cocktails
to the after-dinner liqueur,
décor included!
Open from Valentine's
Day (14 February)
to the end of October

Manufactured in Germany in 1923, Christophe and Jean-Philippe's barge was given to the Allied forces by the Germans as compensation after the war. Today, the barge is home to three nicely decorated bedrooms. Jean-Philippe, a member of Air France's flying personnel, took advantage of his foreign travels to bring back nautical fixtures, such as portholes from old steamships found in depots in Bombay, or plumbing from China that gives the boat a unique atmosphere.

Cabin number 3 has the distinctive feature of possessing a bathtub as well as a bay window at water level opposite the bed – all the better to admire the waves from the moment you awake.

Guests can go on bike rides (the owners will happily loan you bikes) along the nearby towpaths and through the neighbouring vineyards. There are beaches only 10 minutes away, as this part of the Canal du Midi is the closest to the coast.

LES CADOLES DE LA COLLINE DU COLOMBIER

Spectacular modernist cocoons

LES CADOLES DE LA COLLINE DU COLOMBIER 29
La Colline du Colombier
71340 Iguerande
Tel. 06 03 58 30 45
www.troisgros.fr
la-colline-du-colombier@
troisgros.com

ROOMS AND RATES
3 cadoles
Suites for 2 people
2-night minimum
250€ per night

Iguérande's cadoles (named after the old cabins generally built of dry stone that once sheltered wine growers in Burgundy) are spectacular houses on piles, built on a hillside. One of these 3 contemporary homes is suspended in the air; the second, a terrace, fits snugly between two 100-year-old oak trees, and the third is shaded by an apple tree. Guests can live comfortably in all three, since each one is furnished with a large bed, bathroom, small kitchen and a spacious Zen-style living-room that opens onto a balcony overlooking the natural surroundings. The bedrooms are designed like cocoons. Woven hemp covers the ceiling and walls, which seem to blend together to give an incredible effect. This 100% ecological project was conceived by Marie-Pierre and the famous Michael Troisgros, with the help of the no less famous architect Patrick Bouchain. A former adviser to French politician Jack Lang, Bouchain represented France at Venice's Architecture Biennale in 2006. He designed the Zingaro equestrian theatre in Aubervilliers and the "Lieu Unique" in Nantes. Here, the property is also home to an inn housed in a former stable, called "Le Grand Couvert", but you can always go another 15km and dine at Michael Troisgros' gourmet restaurant (3 Michelin stars) in Roanne.

LE CHALET TOURNESOL

A house that rotates, like a sunflower

LE CHALET TOURNESOL ③⓪
Isabelle Mascart
La Pierre
05800 Chauffayer
Tel. 04 92 21 40 98
www.lechalet.biz
contact@lechalet.biz

ROOMS AND RATES
4 B&B rooms
150€ per night
for 2 people,
on half-board
(dinner, room, breakfast,
access to the relaxation
and herb room),
reduced rates for stays
of 2 nights or more
Additional person:
20€ to 35€ on half-board
(free for children under 6)
100€ per night
for 2 people,
breakfast included
(10€ to 15€ for each
additional person)

In April, 2009, Isabelle had the excellent idea to open four guest-rooms in a stunning ecological house that she had built after having discovered the concept: the house is round, made entirely of wood, and rotates so as to capture the most sunlight possible.

Located in a small hamlet near the village of Chauffayer, at an altitude of 950m, the site provides a magnificent view of the mountains of the Écrins massif.

A 4-person jacuzzi can be found in the chalet's annex building.

AU FIL DES BRANCHES

Sleep in a hammock in the trees

AU FIL DES BRANCHES ③
Sylvie Zucco
Ancienne cure, Saint-Nicolas
05260 Saint-Jean-
Saint-Nicolas
Tel. 06 73 50 84 28
www.accompagnateurs-
champsaur.com
Sylvie.zucco@club-internet.fr

ROOMS AND RATES
60€ per person,
includes
half a day of tree-climbing,
accommodation,
and breakfast
40€ per person
for accommodation
and breakfast only
Family rate available
upon request
Children 6 and older allowed
Open May to mid-August,
depending on the weather
(if problems arise,
guests will be removed
to solid shelter)

The "Au Fil des Branches" association offers a rather unusual activity: after showing you how to climb trees, they simply give you the opportunity to spend the night there in a hammock hanging among the leaves.

Kept in balance by two rigid bars along their sides, the hammocks provide a comfortable night's sleep, almost as if you were in a bed. Some people even sleep all curled up! The only uncomfortable position is sleeping on your stomach because of the harness you must wear at all times to avoid the (very minimal) risk of falling in the middle of the night.

Five to a dozen people can be accommodated at a time. Unaccompanied people can join a group.

In the morning, a breakfast of fresh and organic produce is served.

THE NORDIC VILLAGE OF WILLIWAW

Spend the night in an igloo at an altitude of 2300m

**THE NORDIC VILLAGER
OF WILLIWAW** ❷
Philippe Desmurger
05500 Saint-Laurent-du-Cros
Tel. 06 60 68 32 44
www.alpi-traineau.com
ph.desmurger@orange.fr

ROOMS AND RATES
Around 60€ per person
"Cold weather"
sleeping-bag rental: 5€
Open when
the weather allows

At an altitude of 2300m, in the slopes above the Orcières ski resort, Philippe offers to those who aren't overly sensitive to the cold (at night, the temperature can sometimes drop down to -4°F) the chance to experience the true adventure of sleeping in an igloo.

In the late afternoon, by ski lift or by snowshoe, guests climb to the Roche Rousse plateau, before starting on a hike to admire the sunset. If the party is small, a fondue dinner will be served in an igloo (if it's large, you'll dine in a mountainside restaurant – so try to keep your numbers small). Afterwards, it'll be time for a little stargazing (Philippe will help you recognize the constellations) before going to bed.

Contrary to what one might think, the igloos, which can hold a family of 4, have a temperature slightly above 32°F. Comfortably snuggled in a "cold weather" sleeping-bag, you'll likely sleep quite well!

The next day, you can do a little dog-sledding.

It's definitely not to be missed!

THE LE CORBUSIER HOTEL

A unique way to spend the night in a Le Corbusier building

THE LE CORBUSIER HOTEL 🉑
Cité Radieuse
280, boulevard Michelet
13008 Marseille
Tel. 04 91 16 78 00
www.hotellecorbusier.com
contact@
hotellecorbusier.com

ROOMS AND RATES
21 rooms
Rates ranging
from 69€
for a 16m² "cabin"
room with terrace,
sparse but both comfortable
and welcoming,
for those on a small budget,
for "Corbu" aficionados,
98€ for a 32m² studio
with a park view
with 2 balconies
and up to 4 single beds
The large, 32m² rooms
with ocean view are at 135€
Two 32m² studios with
ocean view, 124€
with a nice terrace
and original kitchenette (just
for viewing – not to be used!)
Mini-suite with
ocean view: 135€
Breakfast: 9€
Extra bed: 20€

Almost as famous as the nearby velodrome stadium, Le Corbusier's "Cité Radieuse" (Radiant City), classed as a historic monument, possesses a hotel on the third floor. Unknown to most of Marseille's residents, it was taken over in 2003 by a couple of architecture enthusiasts who redecorated it in the spirit of the period, by reintegrating some of the original furniture and light fixtures and having others reproduced (with the authorization of Charlotte Perriand, who was part of the team). Although the result is true to the original, many clients don't necessarily appreciate the "master's" architecture: the corridors are long, dark and sinister, and the rather sparse décor doesn't really give it the feeling of an up-scale hotel. Situated outside of Marseille's city centre, the site will delight fans of Le Corbusier most of all.

The rest of the building, which is a veritable village in and of itself, is also open to the hotel's clients: a 40-seat cinema, fitness room and sauna, jogging lanes, children's wading pool, and a concert hall on the roof terrace.

From the restaurant's terrace (where breakfast is served), you have a glorious view of the sea and the Frioul Islands.

THE CHÂTEAU VALMER TREE-HOUSE

A tree-house in a vineyard

**THE CHÂTEAU VALMER
TREE-HOUSE 34**
Hôtel Château Valmer
Route de Gigaro
83420 La Croix-Valmer
+33 4 94 55 15 15
www.chateauvalmer.com
info@chateauvalmer.com

ROOMS AND RATES
370€ to 515€
for 2 people,
depending on the season
Another tree-house
for 4 people is also
available: 500€ to 725€
The main hotel's spa
is open to all clients
Open year round

Standing 6m above ground in the branches of an immense 100-year-old oak tree on the Château Valmer estate, the tree-house is a romantic refuge of overwhelming charm. Isolated from the rest of the château in the middle of a vineyard that covers the majority of this 19th-century estate, the tree-house is probably the most beautiful of its kind in France. Only the price might disappoint some. In the summer, you can have a delicious breakfast brought right to the bedroom door. Although you can't see the ocean from the tree-house, it is nevertheless nearby, barely 200m away, at the end of a gorgeous pathway lined by 100-year-old trees.

The beach itself is probably one of the most beautiful and wild beaches along the French Riviera. A few rare buildings, including the annex of the Château Valmer, with a swimming pool and restaurant, make this site a very pleasant place.

On the left, after a second beach with more buildings, a pathway begins along the coast which, after a few hours of walking, will lead you to the Saint-Tropez peninsula. Bought in 1949 by the parents of the current owners, Château Valmer was progressively turned into a 4-star hotel with 42-two rooms, a restaurant, spa, sauna and hammam.

HOTEL WINDSOR

"Each room is a work of art"

HÔTEL WINDSOR ③⑤
11, rue Dalpozzo
06000 Nice
Tel. 04 93 88 59 35
www.hotelwindsornice.com
contact@
hotelwindsornice.com

ROOMS AND RATES
79€ to 155€ in low season;
98€ to 185€ in high season
Breakfast: 12€
Half-board: 32€
Extra bed: 20€
Swimming pool,
relaxation centre
Sauna, hammam and
massages (supplement),
fitness room
Wi-fi
Bar and restaurant
Open year round

Besides being a unique hotel, Hotel Windsor is simply one of the best hotels in Nice: a charming welcome, a beach just a 2-minute walk away, a swimming pool in the garden. And that, of course, is without mentioning that a majority of the rooms have been decorated by artists.

Although the most spectacular room is probably the one Parmiggiani designed as a golden cube with a striped, white bed, other rooms are also interesting.

Those designed by Ben and Joël Ducorroy outshine by their humour and allusions. Charlemagne Palestine, Jean-Pierre Bertrand, Philippe Perrin, François Morellet, Glen Baxter and many others have also given free reign to their imagination. Room 238, designed by Varini, has a unique feature: the graphic coherence of the red line that runs throughout the room, entry and bathroom can only be fully appreciated from one specific spot in the room.

Plan to spend some time exploring to discover all the hotel's secrets.

FRANCIA

OCEANO
ATLANTICO

Mar Cantábrico

A Coruña

1

Santiago de
Compostela

Pontevedra

Vigo

Lugo   Oviedo   Gijón

Santander

Bilbo/
Bilbao   Donostia/
San Sebastián

Biarritz, Bordeaux

2

Ponferrada   León

Gasteiz/
Vitoria   Iruñea/
Pamplona

3

Andorra
La Vella

14

Perpignan

Viana do Castelo

Braga

Ourense

Bragança

Burgos   Logroño

4 **5**

Soria

ara o a

Lleida/
Lérida

12

G
G

Porto

15

Vila Real

Zamora

Valladolid

Viseu

Salamanca

Segovia

Barcelona

11

Figueira
da Foz

16

Guarda

Ávila

Tarragona

Coimbra

Leiria

MADRID

6

Santarém   Castelo Branco

Cáceres

7

Toledo

Castellón de la Plana

Estoril

LISBOA

Badajoz

Mérida

Ciudad
Real

8

e r e l

Valencia

Mallorca

Palma

Beja

Valdepeñas

Albacete

Ibiza

Eivissa

10

Islas Baleares

Cabre

Formentera

Córdoba

Jaén

Alicante

Elche

Lagos

Faro   Huelva

Sevilla

Granada

9

Murcia

Cartagena

OCEANO
ATLANTICO

Cádiz

Málaga

Almería

MAR MEDITERRANEO

Tarifa

Gibraltar

Estrecho de Gibraltar

Ceuta

ÁFRICA

0   50   100

I la anaria

OCEANO
ATLANTICO

Lanzarote

La Palma

San a r
de la al a

San a r
de eneri e

La al a
de ran anari a

Arre i e

er o
del o ari o

Gomera

Tenerife

Fuerteventura

Hierro   0   40 km

Gran Canaria

l A

SPAIN AND PORTUGAL

O SEMÁFORO

Stay at the far reaches of the world

O Semáforo ❶
Faro de Finisterre s/n
15155 Finisterre (A
Coruña), Spain
+34 981 725 869
osemaforo@msn.com
www.osemaforo.com

ROOMS AND RATES

In the low season, the rate for a double room is €95 and €50 for a single. In the mid-season (1–30 June and 1 September to 31 October), a double room costs €105 and a single room €55. In July and August, during Holy Week and at Christmas (20 December to 7 January), the price of a double room is €110 and €60 for a single (7% VAT included). Additional bed available for €12. Breakfast not included (€6.20 per person). Closed November.

DIRECTIONS

From A Coruña (La Coruña), take the AP55 to Carballo where you pick up the C552 towards Vimianzo, Corcubión and finally Finisterre. Pass through the village and head towards the Finisterre Lighthouse (Faro de Finisterre). From Santiago de Compostela, head towards A Coruña on the AP9 then change to the AP6 towards Carballo and follow the route indicated above. You can also take the C1914 towards Portomouro and Berdolas and join the C552 towards Finisterre.

Finis Terrae (*Fisterra* in Galician), the last point before the vast immensity of the Atlantic, has always been a magical place. Today, this enclave of the Coruña coast still echoes with pagan legends and shipwrecks and shines with the most amazing sunsets on the planet. If that's not enough to convince you to come all the way to what was considered for centuries as the end of the earth, Fisterra offers some of the most unique accommodation in all of Spain: O Semáforo. At 143 m (470 ft) above sea level, near the emblematic Finisterre Lighthouse, stands a former military guardpost that has been home to a charming five-room hotel since 1999. Its name refers to the origins of this unique edifice that, from the late nineteenth century and until the construction of the lighthouse, communicated with ships from its privileged location using signal flags. It was also used as a meteorological base until the army abandoned it forty years ago and it sank into oblivion.

Then, between 1997 and 1999, the Ministry of Tourism of the Autonomous Community and the Regional Council of Galicia restored the building and converted it into an inviting hotel that offers unequalled sensations.

Other than its exceptional location at the westernmost point of the peninsula, the main characteristic of O Semáforo is the infinite presence of the ocean. Staying in this hotel, with the ocean on all sides, is like taking an Atlantic boat trip without moving an inch.

The omnipresence of the ocean is felt in a thousand ways. The smell of saltpetre impregnates every nook and cranny, especially at sunrise and sunset when the copper and reddish tones reflect upon the walls and through the windows. "The ocean catches us from all sides and its recognisable odour infiltrates the entire structure, especially in winter when the waves break violently and the wind brings the sea spray up to the building," describes Desiderio, who is in charge of making sure guests feel at home here. Many of them are exhausted pilgrims who end their pilgrimage to Compostela here. Staying at O Semáforo is a unique experience, especially in winter when the coast is beaten by storms.

The completely symmetrical architecture of the hotel resembles that of the Finisterre Lighthouse, where lighthouse keepers still work. On foggy days, the impressive foghorn (which locals call the "cow") sounds throughout the bay and warns boats of the proximity of the coast. On such foggy, cold days, enjoying a hot cup of tea and a good book in the second-floor living room is a true hedonist pleasure.

It's also the opportunity to taste seafood and fresh fish at one of the six tables reserved for hotel guests, where traditional Galician cuisine is served.

The rooms are comfortable, inviting and decorated with simplicity. The second-floor rooms are a little smaller and have three windows, while those on the third floor have a sloping ceiling and large skylights that allow you to stargaze when the sky is clear. All the rooms provide magnificent ocean views. So, you have a dilemma: should you opt for a room overlooking the Ria de Corcubión and the impressive Monte Pindo, or one overlooking the sea? That means choosing between a magnificent dawn and a melancholy sunset.

It's a difficult decision that could become the perfect excuse for a return trip to enjoy yet again this place "where the earth ends, and the ocean, which never ends, upsets and seduces", as Nobel Literature prizewinner and Galician Camilo José Cela writes.

SILKEN GRAN HOTEL DOMINE BILBAO

Mirror image of the Guggenheim

SILKEN GRAN HOTEL DOMINE BILBAO ❷
Alameda Mazarredo 61
48009 Bilbao, Spain
+34 944 253 300
recepcion.domine@
hoteles-silken.com
www.hoteles-silken.com

ROOMS AND RATES
From €117 per night
131 rooms and fourteen suites

DIRECTIONS
The hotel is just 15 km
(9 miles) from the city
centre. If you arrive by
plane, take the Bizkaibus
Aeropuerto-Bilbao bus
as far as the Alameda de
Recalde stop. The closest
metro station is Moyúa.

The cosmopolitan city of Bilbao, which is always open to new trends, is home to two of the most avant-garde buildings in Spain: the Guggenheim museum, by Frank Gehry, and the Gran Hotel Domine, a marvellous five-star hotel entirely designed by Javier Mariscal. It's the only 100% designer hotel in Spain. Inaugurated eight years ago – by Sofía Loren and Diana Ross, no less –, its fabulous architecture makes it one of the most spectacular designer hotels in the world. The interior of the hotel, just like the exterior, is in constant harmony with the museum: the interior decor pays homage to twentieth-century design and to designers like Philippe Starck, Le Corbusier, Mies van del Rohe and Alvar Aalto. "When you walk through the various rooms of the hotel, you feel as if the collection of furniture you're admiring could be found in a modern art museum," explains Fracisco Javier Campuzano, the hotel manager. Everything – from the staff uniforms, stationery and linens, to the exact placement of each object – was designed by Mariscal in collaboration with interior decorator Fernando Salas. It's a monumental work of art transformed into an impressive hotel, where unpretentious luxury is the mainstay. On entering you're struck by the atrium, which fully illuminates the interior with the light that floods through its glass roof. "Light is one of the most surprising elements of the hotel. Indeed, it is difficult to obtain such luminosity in a city like Bilbao," remarks Salas. He believes this bath of light has a positive influence on the mood of the clients who are "principally lovers of art and design". Of course, the *Ciprés Fósil* sculpture doesn't go unnoticed. It's a huge sculpture by Mariscal (26 m / 85 ft tall and weighing 90 tons) that occupies the entire height of the hotel, from ground floor to terrace. Don't miss a visit to the terrace with its view of the Guggenheim in the upper part of the hotel, in the glass cupola that crowns the atrium. Lounging in a deckchair across from the museum's organic silhouette, you've got the best perspective from which to attest to the veracity of Gehry's declaration that "in the night wind, its titanium skin seems to breathe".

AIRE DE BARDENAS

Windows overlooking a field of wheat

AIRE DE BARDENAS ❸
Ctra. de Ejea, Km 1.5
31500 Tudela (Navarra), Spain
+34 948 11 66 66
info@hotelaire.com
www.airedebardenas.com

ROOMS AND RATES
Twenty-two rooms
(including four suites)
From €165 for a double
room with private patio,
€225 for the "outdoor cube"
with patio and outdoor
bath, and €290 for the
suite with private patio.

DIRECTIONS
From Zaragoza (Saragossa)
or Logroño, take motorway
AP-68, then exit 18 towards
Tudela. At the roundabout,
follow Parque Natural
de Bardenas. Then take
motorway A-68 towards
Zaragoza (without entering
the city) and exit 98
(Tudela Sur). Finally, turn
right towards Ejea de los
Caballeros on the NA-125.

The *cierzo*, a wind from the north-west that blows through the Bardenas Reales de Navarra, violently lashes the wheat fields in the middle of which stands the Aire de Bardenas hotel. This four-star hotel is located near the nature reserve, a barren paradise that resembles Arizona more than the northern part of the peninsula, just 3 km (2 miles) from the town of Tudela.

The hotel opens onto a unique landscape, as serene as it is austere, that invites you to relax as, comfortably settled in your room, you let your eyes wander. When you wake in the morning to contemplate this landscape of the arid Bardenas on one side and the irrigated fields of the Ribera Tudelana and the Ebro on the other, you'll understand. Thanks to its light architecture, the hotel blends in with the landscape, just like the region's agricultural structures. Peace, nature and design are the key words to describe this avant-garde construction by architects Mónica Rivera and Emiliano López.

The hotel's originality lies in its curious habitable windows. In fact, the rooms are protected patios that give you the feeling of being outdoors (or perhaps it's the outdoors that is creeping into the room?). The windows serve, in turn, as sofas, an extra bed, or a corner where you can read, take a nap, or watch TV on one of the built-in screens.

Another distinctive feature is the large double bath in one of the suites, and then there's the metal bathtub on the patio of one of the cubes. "We offer our guests these unique and luxurious services so they can fully enjoy the rural atmosphere, the austere beauty that surrounds the hotel, and the mystic nature of the Bardenas landscape," states Natalia Pérez, the hotel manager and owner.

MARQUÉS DE RISCAL

A stunning Gehry-designed hotel

Hotel Marqués de Riscal ❹
Calle Torrea, 1
Elciego 01340
Spain
+34 945 180880
reservations.
marquesderiscal@
luxurycollection.com
www.luxurycollection.com

ROOMS AND RATES
Forty-three rooms and suites.
From €300 for a grand deluxe
room in low season to €850
in high season, exclusive of
VAT but including breakfast.
Suites are from €350 to
€1,095 with the luxurious
Gehry suite in addition.

LOCATION
Elciego is about
112 km (70 miles) south
of the city of Bilbao.

A roofline of shimmering ribbons of pink, gold and silver titanium, the hotel Marqués de Riscal in the northern Spanish town of Elciego echoes the Gehry Associates trademark architecture found in the Guggenheim Bilbao and Bridge of Life building in Panama. The hotel was originally conceived as a twenty-first-century wine chateau in the Rioja Alavesa grape-growing region. It has been transformed into Frank O. Gehry's only hotel project to date.

Vinos de los Herederos de Marqués de Riscal is recognized as a pioneer in winemaking and the hotel is a futuristic beacon rising above the classical stone architecture of the town and the surrounding vineyards to highlight the growth in fortunes of the Rioja wine region as a whole.

The main Gehry-designed hotel has forty-three rooms and is stunning in every respect, both externally and internally, with designer furniture and hi-tech gadgets. There are also a number of more traditional, utilitarian rooms in an annex, connected to Hotel Marqués de Riscal by a bridge, where the spa and pool are located. Although the annex rooms have views of the vineyard and artistic furnishings, they lack the outrageous charm of the main building.

There are two restaurants in the hotel: "1860" and the more formal Marqués de Riscal restaurant which is closed on Mondays. While there have been mixed reviews for the more formal restaurant, the executive chef is the Michelin-starred Francis Paniego, so an average meal is unlikely and the wines will most certainly be exceptional.

The spa itself is worthy of mention for it provides wine therapy treatments using products made from grape extracts, created exclusively by Caudalíe Vinothérapie. It has received many awards for the treatments and venue. Now you can see, drink and be beautified with Rioja grapes.

Managed by Starwood Hotels and Resorts brand, "The Luxury Collection" Hotel Marqués de Riscal may appear a little out of the way, but is well worth the detour to take in the stunning design and wine-themed spa.

HOTEL VIURA

Unconventional design in the vineyards

HOTEL VIURA ❺
Calle Mayor s/n
01307 Villabuena de
Álava (Álava), Spain
+34 945 609 000
info@hotelviura.com
www.hotelviura.com

ROOMS AND RATES
The hotel has thirty-three
rooms on three floors:
thirteen Viura (standard)
rooms, fourteen deluxe
rooms and six suites. The
rate for a Viura room, for
two people, varies from €110
to €255; those of the deluxe
rooms and the suites vary
from €130 to €300 and €190
to €440, respectively. The
price does not include VAT.
A continental breakfast is
included. The rooms have a
private bar with a selection
of La Rioja wines; the
non-alcoholic drinks are free.

DIRECTIONS
The hotel is located 40 km
(25 miles) from Logroño,
44 km (27 miles) from
Vitoria and 111 km (69 miles)
from Burgos and Bilbao.
From Logroño, take the A124
to Samaniego then follow the
signs to Villabuena de Álava.
From Vitoria, take the A2124
to the intersection with the
A124 then follow the signs.
The hotel is after Eliza Plaza.

The 300 or so inhabitants of Villabuena de Álava, a little village nestled in an ocean of vineyards at the heart of Rioja de Álava, are truly privileged. Indeed, they enjoy the tranquil rhythm of a 100% wine-growing village, all while having the chance to contemplate the veritable work of art that is the designer four-star Hotel Viura, which opened to the public in March 2010. Created by the Designhouses firm that owns the hotel, Viura is striking for its modern architecture and innovative design that nevertheless blends perfectly into the rural environment of the village. Formed by a superposition of cubes, its façade is a kaleidoscope of shapes and colours where chaos seems to reign, creating an incredible play of light. Just a few steps from this explosion of design, the Plaza Mayor and San Andrés Church, built between 1538 and 1728 juxtaposed against the church, create a striking contrast of styles and periods. As the locals say, when you look at the façade straight on, the hotel resembles a bunch of grapes lying on the hill of Villabuena de Álava village. Beyond its architectural virtuosity, Viura is a unique hotel where every nook and cranny seems to evoke the surrounding wine-growing environment. First of all, its name, 'viura', is that of a grape typically used to produce white wine in the Rioja Alavesa region. What's more, staves hang from the ceilings of the corridors, the room numbers are written in chalk as in old wine cellars, and the ceiling of the Restaurant Viura is covered with old wine barrels.

We suggest choosing one of the ten rooms on the top floor that have a private terrace, where guests can enjoy this magnificent environment into which the hotel seems to disappear. But this is not the only viewpoint from which your eyes can wander. One of the most wonderful places is the lounge on the top floor, where a landscaped terrace offers spectacular views of the surrounding areas. Admiring the sunset over a delicious glass of wine becomes a true pleasure.

HOTEL PUERTA AMÉRICA

Every floor a different design adventure

HOTEL PUERTA AMÉRICA ❻
Avenida de América, 41
28002 Madrid
Spain
+34 917 445 400
hotel.puertamerica@
hoteles-silken.com
www.hotelpuertamerica.com

ROOMS AND RATES
342 bedrooms.
The Hotel Puerta América
has 342 bedrooms including
a number of suites on the
twelfth floor. You should
expect to pay around €360
for a double room plus 7%
tax excluding breakfast.

LOCATION
The hotel is midway between
the airport and the city
centre and is not in the
centre of town. A taxi from
the airport should cost
around €15, and around €10
into town. Alternatively
consider the metro stop next
to the hotel, but be prepared
to change a couple of times
to get into the centre.

With twelve floors and communal spaces providing a unique style designed by nineteen design agencies, your choice of room is critical at Hotel Puerta América. Thankfully the front-desk staff anticipate guests changing rooms. A menu of design choices for the different floors is provided at check-in and you are recommended to study closely, or to review the website in advance. Some floors are a triumph of style over substance and there are stories of guests whose frustration in trying to dim the walls or use hi-tech appliances forced them to change rooms. Although floors have a similar layout, when you leave the elevator on each floor you feel in altogether different worlds – from futuristic red plastic to black marble through to traditional leather and wood. Examples include the first floor by Zaha Hadid, where everything seems to come out from the wall. The bathroom is a single structure from floor to ceiling, which changes colour according to the room. Most frustratingly, the waste basket is a challenge for guests because it's not so easy to find. Or you can just drop your rubbish on the floor ... The eighth floor by Kathryn Findlay, "Light in Motion", intends to suggest a feminine touch. Refusing to consider walls or doors, Findlay provided for sweeping white curtains that separate the bathroom from the room. The entire room is white and forms a single space.

Patience is required on the ninth floor with Richard Gluckman's "Boxes of Colours" concept as you need to look for everything, all hidden in boxes. The biggest box, in the middle of the room, houses the TV. In the bathroom, the first thing you see when you enter is a large glass box containing the shower, with a sliding door separating it from the bedroom and a white metal curtain. A raw industrial look contrasts with back-lit illumination, so don't forget to ask how to turn off the lights otherwise you'll struggle to get to sleep.

With every floor a different artistic design, this hotel challenges the senses in an architectural assault course of design.

CASA RURAL

Sleep under the stars of Extremadura's la dehesa*

CASA RURAL ❼
Plaza Mayor 8
10163 Aldea del Cano
(Cáceres), Spain
+34 666 431 420
info@crviadelaplata.com
www.crviadelaplata.com

ROOMS AND RATES
The "Sleep under the Stars" package offers a three-day, two-night stay in Extremadura's *la dehesa* for €129 per person. The package includes cottage accommodation, a night under the stars, full board, and daytime and evening activities. From spring to summer. Groups of eight to ten.

DIRECTIONS
Aldea del Cano is located halfway between Mérida and Cáceres on the A66. For the "Dormir bajo las Estrellas" ("Sleep under the Stars") package, you must first go to the Vía de la Plata cottage in the centre of the village.

To sleep in a comfortable bed lost in an ocean of holm oaks under thousands of stars is an invitation that no curious person who appreciates extraordinary accommodation would refuse. A utopia, you say? This dream became reality in 2010 thanks to the initiative of Teresa Gutiérrez, owner of the Vía de la Plata cottage, a building typical of the farms of Aldea del Cano, in the Sierra de Montáchez y Tamuja region. The "Sleep under the Stars" concept is as simple as it is inviting: to spend the night in the largest hotel in the world – Extremadura's *la dehesa*. There is no lack of advantages to this new type of accommodation, created to allow guests to enjoy the pure essence of part of Spain's ecological richness, the fruit of nature and the work of man. "I decided to bring this project to life in order to introduce people to *la dehesa*, this Mediterranean forest that is Extremadura's greatest asset. We wouldn't be here without it," explains Teresa, who describes how she got the idea for this project. "We'd been running the cottage for ten years and, one day, we decided to bring the beds outside to enjoy the cottage in a different way! It was no sooner said than done." The "Sleep under the Stars" package allows guests to admire the marvels of *la dehesa* from all angles for three days and two nights. "We have to have a group of eight to ten people because the logistics required to set up the room outdoors are extensive. It's just not feasible for one or two couples, even if the idea is quite romantic," explains Teresa. "We still use the cottage as a base if the weather keeps the guests from sleeping in this thousand-year-old forest. On the first night, we welcome the guests in the cottage, where they are lodged in one of the comfortable double rooms. The next morning, their introduction to the universe of *la dehesa* begins with a visit to one of the surrounding farms, then a tasting in the ham drying sheds where they discover the curing of Iberian ham, and finally walks along the natural paths. On the second night, we dine and sleep in the middle of the plain, in this paradise that we have explored and come to know during the day. The centre of this 'room without walls', designed for an extraordinary night, is a large, comfortable bed protected by a mosquito Everything is set up so that nothing will perturb your sleep. A small table with chairs complete the furnishings of this most unusual room. *La dehesa* does the rest with the background noise and various nocturnal aromas: oak, cork, humid ground. The night sounds are impressive, as they envelop everything."

Nevertheless, the "Sleep under the Stars" experience is more than just a peaceful and passive night outdoors. At night, there are other ways to discover the plain: night-time walks in the countryside with a guide to interpret the sounds of local wildlife, or the telling of local legends in the shadow of the holm oaks. But that's not all. The most popular activity is star-gazing. An astronomy specialist points out the different constellations and names some of the stars with which guests will spend the night. At daybreak, a hearty breakfast awaits on a long table set up under the oaks and which serves as the dining room. This early morning meal, like the other meals served during the stay, is delicious and typical of Extremadura cuisine. As with any country meal, it includes a selection of local products. It's a delicious and original way to crown this extraordinary sleeping experience.

la dehesa, from the Latin term *defesa*, designates a plot of land generally used for grazing

HOTEL PLAZA DE TOROS DE ALMADÉN

A night in the arena

HOTEL PLAZA DE TOROS DE ALMADÉN ❽
Plaza Waldo Ferrer, s/n
13400 Almadén
(Ciudad Real), Spain
+34 926 264 333
almaden@estancias.com
www.hotelplazadetoros.com

ROOMS AND RATES
The rates vary depending on the season. Prices, which include breakfast, vary from €57.78 for a double room in low season to €161.57 for the suite in high season.

DIRECTIONS
From Madrid, take the N420, then the CM415 through Saceruela. You can also take the C424 from Ciudad Real towards Almadenejos. From Cordoba, take the N502 which passes through Santa Eufemia.

In August 1752, Almadén had to find a way to put an end to the high mortality rate of the prisoners working in the mercury mines, as well as the epidemics that spread throughout the population. The city didn't have a hospital to treat the sick. So, the Superintendant of the Mines, Don Francisco Javier de Villegas, had twenty-four independent lodgings built, which avoided having to put several families in one house while also creating a way to finance the construction of a Miners' Hospital by using the rental revenue. The twenty-four houses formed hexagonal arenas that could be used to organise bullfighting events.

This is the unique history of the Hotel Plaza de Toros de Almadén, the only hotel in the world located around hexagonal arenas. In addition to the twenty-three rooms around the Bull Square, where bullfights are still held today, the hotel has inherited other period characteristics: white stone arches, a tiled roof, and other wooden and stone elements dating from the original construction. All the rooms, with the exception of the suite, are oriented

towards the exterior of the arena, so only the window of the suite provides a view of the arenas, but unfortunately not during the bullfights. Indeed, you can't enjoy the show from this privileged viewpoint because additional bleachers are set up around the exterior gallery.

The rooms all have TV, air conditioning, a mini-bar, internet access and bathroom. The decor is rather rustic with whitewashed walls and bare wooden doors with forged iron nails. To appreciate the uniqueness of the arenas, you should quickly set down your luggage and walk around the exterior gallery which gives you a view of the entire enclosure. Then, as there isn't a bull in sight, don't hesitate to head down into the arena to walk for your first and perhaps last time on the sand of a real bullfighting arena.

The Arenas of Almadén were occupied by residents until quite recently – the last of them left the site in the 1990s. After careful remodelling, the hotel opened its doors in 2003, and the first bullfight was held just a year later. Two of the must-see sites of the hotel are the bullfighting museum and the restaurant, which is the best place to take a break between two "*tercios*" (the bullfights are divided into three parts, or *tercios*) and enjoy a few local specialities, such as oxtail tortillas with tomato sauce.

If you're interested in combining a stay at the hotel with a bullfight, your only chance is during Holy Week and the local festivals in August. Of course, the demand for these dates is quite high so you have to reserve far in advance to avoid disappointment. For several hours, the bubbling excitement of the banderilleros, picadors, matadors and richly-coloured accompaniment to the bullfighting teams animates the calm that generally reigns over the depths of the arenas. All this hustle and bustle undoubtedly helps visitors feel like a torero, at least for a day.

CUEVAS PEDRO ANTONIO DE ALARCÓN

For 21st-century troglodytes

CUEVAS PEDRO ANTONIO DE ALARCÓN ❾
Bda. de San Torcuato, S/N
18500 Guadix
(Granada), Spain
+34 958 664 986
cavehotel@infonegocio.com
www.cuevaspedroantonio.es

ROOMS AND RATES
From €70 for two people.

DIRECTIONS
From Granada, take the A92 motorway to the Guadix-Benalúa de Guadix exit. The exit joins up with a local road about 2 km (1 mile) from the town of Guadix. The cave houses of Pedro Antonio de Alarcón are located 250 m (300 yards) after the level crossing.

Guadix is a town in the province of Granada where nearly half the population live in caves carved out of the age-old stone, the geological origin of which is the decomposition of a glacier that once covered the entire valley.

The inhabitants of this region have built their homes in these types of cave since the sixteenth century. The best way to experience this return to the stone age – with all the comforts that our ancestors never had – is to head for the locality around Guadix where Pedro Antonio de Alarcón's cave houses are to be found. This ensemble of caves converted into apartments was once a neighbourhood of Guadix. Its reddish clay mounds create a lunar landscape against which the façades and whitewashed chimneys stand out. At sunset, from the terraces of the cave houses, the contrast of colours between the claystone, the whiteness of the lime, and the blue of the sky transforms the troglodyte homes of Pedro Antonio de Alarcón into a palette of blinding colour.

The story began twenty years ago when the owners decided to buy the cave houses from their former occupants

in order to create a complex of twenty-three apartments. Each includes an equipped kitchen, a combined dining and living room with TV, a bathroom and, depending on the size of the cave, one or two bedrooms. Some are suitable for a single guest while others can accommodate up to eight.

In both the rigours of winter and the heat of summer, the claystone helps to maintain a constant and pleasant temperature.

ISLA TAGOMAGO

A private paradise in the Mediterranean

ISLA TAGOMAGO ❿
07480 Santa Eulàlia
(Ibiza), Spain
+34 971 228 019
info@tagomago-island.com
www.tagomago-island.com

ROOMS AND RATES
€100,000 to €250,000 per
week depending on dates.
Five double suites for up to
ten people; price includes a
staff of four (chef, assistant
chef, maid and captain for
boat and water sports),
catering and the round trip
to Ibiza by helicopter.

DIRECTIONS
The island is located less
than a kilometre from
the Ibiza coast. You can
get there by private boat
from Santa Eulàlia marina
or by helicopter.

One of the most exclusive refuges in Spain and all the Mediterranean lies 900 m off Ibiza: the heavenly island of Tagomago, one of the rare, but also one of the most beautiful, private islands of the Iberian Peninsula.

Truly wealthy clients (from €100,000 per week) no longer have to go all the way to the Caribbean or the Indian Ocean. The island, for rent since 2008, has welcomed tabloid celebrities, members of the European jet set, athletes, businessmen, politicians and artists from the world over. Staying at Tagomago is more than just an idyllic vacation: in this exclusive enclave, the site gives you a true feeling of absolute freedom.

The only inhabitable construction on the island is a superb designer villa. Recently renovated, it holds five double suites, each with their own terrace. A marvellous swimming pool overlooking the sea, a LED lighting system that brings all the magic of Ibiza to the island, a garden, an outdoor jacuzzi, a luxurious relaxation space with couches, and a gym on the terrace that provides unrestricted views complete the description of this dream house.

CIRCO MUSEO RALUY

Sleep over and enjoy the greatest show on Earth!

CIRCO MUSEO RALUY ⓫
Ctra. de Tortosa km 1 s/n
43896 Aldea
(Tarragona), Spain
+34 609 321207 /
+34 609 326330
info@raluy.com
www.raluy.com

ROOMS AND RATES
The gypsy caravan
(maximum six people)
houses a bedroom with
double bed, a small living
room with TV, a bedroom
with two additional beds,
and a full bath. It has heating
and air conditioning, as
well as a free mini bar with
coffee and herbal tea. A stay
in the caravan costs €200
per night in the double
room (€50 extra for each
additional bed). The price
of the accommodation
includes entry to the show.

DIRECTIONS
The circus travels throughout
Spain. The best way to find
out where it is, and thus
where you can stay, is to
consult its website. You'll
find a list of all the cities
on the current tour.

For all children great and small ... Come in, look around and above all settle in for a comfortable stay in one of the most traditional Spanish circuses!

Since 2010, the Raluy circus museum has invited guests to stay in its "Hotel on wheels", a wooden gypsy caravan from the early twentieth century that gives you a glimpse into the world of the circus. To be exact, let yourself be transported by the magic of this traditional circus, where the true artists aren't the animals but the tightrope walkers, knife throwers and clowns.

The Raluy circus is the ideal place to immerse yourself in this life of travel and to realise what a life dedicated to entertainment means. Winner of the National Circus Award in 1996 (given by the Ministry of Education and Culture) and of the Creu de Sant Jordi Award in 2006 (awarded by the Autonomous Government of Catalonia), Raluy is not just a circus, it's also a museum – a fragment of itinerant history, as illustrated by the wooden caravans and wagons of various origins: Romania, Czech Republic, England and Germany. These are genuine works of art that Luis and Carlos Raluy, brothers and owners of the circus, have restored and adapted to our era, while carefully respecting their original nineteenth- and twentieth-century appearance. Staying in one of these caravans undoubtedly gives you the feeling of belonging to the forty-strong group who make up the extended Raluy family. It's a unique experience you won't easily forget. Indeed, circus fans and the curious-minded will all discover what a day in the life of these performers is like: dare to serve as a target for Silvano, the knife thrower; help Steacy the tightrope walker prepare her freestanding ladder routine; or watch Sandro the clown as he applies his make-up backstage. Enjoy it all without giving up the comfort of the 1939 showman caravan, where all guests stay. Spending a night here is like travelling back in time and rediscovering the ambiance of legendary circuses.

However, sleeping in the circle of caravans isn't the only highlight of this experience. The guests of the "Hotel on Wheels" also take part in the show, either before (children love participating in circus chores like the rehearsals or welcoming the audience) or during the show under the big top. "Guests have a reserved seat in the VIP stand and they are generally chosen as volunteers for the acrobatic or comic routines," explains William Giribaldi, an acrobat and manager of the caravan. The itinerary life of a circus doesn't mean giving up on comfort. The 25 m² caravan holds everything you'll need: a full bath, a living room with TV, and good comfortable beds where you can dream of countless incredible acrobatic feats, tomfoolery and popcorn!

CABANES ALS ARBRES

Sleep perched in a tree

CABANES ALS ARBRES ⑫
Carretera de Vallclara s/n
17403 Sant Hilari
Sacalm, Spain
+34 625 411 409
info@cabanesalsarbres.com
www.cabanesalsarbres.com

ROOMS AND RATES
From €97 to €117 per night
Ten treehouses

DIRECTIONS
From Barcelona, heading
towards Vic, take the C25 in
the direction of Girona. At
exit 202, take the road Plà de
les Arenes towards Sant Hilari
Sacalm. At the crossroads
before you reach the village,
head towards Sant Sandurní
d'Osomort. The Vallclara road
(or lane) that leads directly to
the treehouses is 3 km (about
2 miles) ahead on the right.

At the heart of the Sierra del Montseny, 84 km (52 miles) from Barcelona, you can rediscover your childhood dreams and live in a cabin in the treetops: the *Cabanes als arbres* are cabins hanging 10 m above the ground attached to the trunks of robust Douglas firs. Dutchman Karin van Veen and Frenchman Manu Grymonpré are the originators of this new type of accommodation in Spain. The masterminds behind other nature adventure parks, they have a clear idea of the site's philosophy: "Our goal is to offer the pleasure of spending a night with a tree and its ecosystem, while teaching people about the importance of the environment." The first two treehouses were inaugurated in July 2009, and today there are ten: six 2-person cabins and four 4-person cabins. Once checked in, you're overcome by the feeling of living a childhood adventure. The cabins built in the trees of Montseny have no ground supports. "They are attached to the tree by several cables to divide the weight." Entrance is by a suspended bridge or a ladder. All the cabins are made from wood (even the handles on the windows) and are built around the trunk. They are each 30 m² with a terrace of 10 m². The interior, through which the trunk passes vertically, is furnished with a double bed, sofa, table and chairs; there's a "bathroom" area with jugs of water and a dry toilet.

The real life of a twenty-first-century Robinson Crusoe comes with its own challenges. The treehouses have no electricity (Karin and Manu provide candles and torches) and no running water, but a short distance away at Mas La Vileta (which also offers rooms for €57 to €67, depending on the season), is the reception area where all amenities are located, including showers, toilets, a magnificent swimming pool and a restaurant.

LES COLS PAVELLONS

An architectural poem, a Zen experience

LES COLS PAVELLONS ⓭
Av. Mas les Cols 2
17800 Olot (Girona), Spain
+34 699 813 817
lescols@lescolspavellons.com
www.lescolspavellons.com

ROOMS AND RATES
There are five villas. The rate per night for two people is €275 (breakfast and picnic included; VAT not included). Breakfast and the picnic are essentially made up of regional products. The breakfast, which is served in the villa, includes tea, coffee, homemade jam on "pan de coca" –a Catalonian bread recipe, La Fageda yogurt, Can Papot sausages, and Mas Farró cheese. Check-in beginning at 3pm. For lunch at Les Cols restaurant, please reserve by phone (972 26 92 09) or e-mail (lescols@lescols.com).

DIRECTIONS
Les Cols Pavellons is located in the town of Olot, in Girona province. From Barcelona, take the AP7 towards Girona, then the 8 (Besalú-Olot) and the C66 which leads to Olot. Take the Olot Norte exit then, at the roundabout, the third exit. Another option is to take the Bracons tunnel, then the C17 to Vic where you follow the C37 all the way to Olot. After going through the town, take the Canya road. From the centre of Spain, by Zaragoza and Lleida (Lérida), the road passes through Artesa de Segre (C1313), Solsona (L301), Berga (C149) and Ripoll before arriving at Olot.

Mystery, peace, sky, sobriety, silence … but also unreality, weightlessness, earth, and beyond all of that, a void as the point of departure for a voyage of the soul. That's what Les Cols Pavellons inspires, an extremely rare concept that transcends the notion of a hotel itself to become a metaphysical experience.

Located near the twelfth-century *mas* (house or farm) that houses the futuristic restaurant Les Cols (two Michelin stars) of female chef Fina Puigdevall, the five villas that won the FAD-06 architectural award are built of glass and steel, a combination of materials that offers guests a sensorial, initiatory and Zen experience.

Staying here causes you to lose all notion of the traditional hotel experience, which is why time spent here leads to very extreme impressions: you either love it or hate it! For example, when you enter the glass villa, you're struck by the asceticism of the furniture (there are no chairs and the closet comprising the bathrobe, soap and mini bar is hidden in the structure). So you wonder where the bed is. Well, there isn't one … at least not until evening, when the geometric platform that sits imposingly in the bedroom is transformed into a bed by the hotel staff. In other words, a stay here requires taking on a new perception of the use of space. Another surprise is the fact that the toilet and sink aren't traditional. There is no tap in the rectangular steel sink, yet when it detects a presence water starts to run out as if from the soft current of a stream; nearby, there's a shower with a pebble floor and a bathtub-pool that is always full and ready. The moral is: the void is the master of the house. "It's a way to spend the night in communion with the outdoors, with the sky but also with the earth, an experience that you can liken to sleeping under the stars, even if here it is filtered by the prism of architecture, which asks for us to become aware of strange and moving things that were nevertheless natural for our ancestors," explains

Judit Planella, owner of Les Cols Pavellons and a key player in the ritual that precedes a guest's entry to the villa. It's a sort of welcome ceremony similar to an initiatory ritual during which Judit receives guests in the *non-reception*, a dark room where volcanic earth crunches under your feet and candles illuminate cabbages which, as the totemic vegetables of the hotel, preside over this opening ceremony as if it were an ancestral rite.

"It's a transition between the exterior and the interior that allows you to divest yourself of all material things so you're ready to receive the sensations and experiences we offer," explains Judit, transformed into a veritable oracle. Enveloped in the light of the sky, the guests are guided to their rooms by a futuristic reed plantation of green-coloured steel. The privacy of these glass caves – from 20 m^2 to 30 m^2 in size – is ensured by green-tinted glass slats that let you glimpse of the interior courtyards (the mortar floor imitates the undulations of the volcanic lava of La Garrotxa) of each room. The layout of the villas is reminiscent of the linear structure of a traditional vegetable garden, a native heritage that, like a synalepha, fusions with the latent Japanese culture.

Zen is à la mode in Olot. In the villa there is no television, so conversation and dialogue with your inner self are an inevitable rite of passage. In this environment, and especially at night, you realise everything silence has to offer: listen to the relaxing murmur of the water babbling in the pool, or fall asleep while admiring the sparkling stars unveiled through the roof above the bed.

ACTIVITIES
You can explore the volcanic countryside of the La Garrotxa region or enter the magical beech forests of La Fageda d'en Jordà, which are rooted in the lava flow of the Croscat volcano. You can also stroll through the old town of Sant Pau, discover the beautiful La Vall d'en Bas valley or head off to climb the Montascopa volcano and enjoy the views from its summit.

IGLÚ HOTEL GRANDVALIRA

Sleep like an Eskimo

IGLÚ HOTEL GRANDVALIRA ⓴
Coma III – Edificio Xiruxuca
Grandvalira – Grau
Roig, Andorra
+376 891 800
reserves@grandvalira.com
www.grandvalira.com

ROOMS AND RATES
From €310 per night.
Open from 25 November to
mid-April, depending on the
meteorological conditions
and closing of the station
Five igloo rooms
of 25 m² each
Four Standard or
Romantic rooms
One Romantic suite

DIRECTIONS
There are two ways to drive
to Andorra from Spain:
highway C145 from Lleida
and highway C16 from the
Cadí tunnel or Puigcerdà. La
Seu d'Urgell is located 30 km
(about 20 miles) from the
first access road to the slopes,
Encamp. You can also travel
by AVE (high-speed train)
from Madrid or Barcelona to
Lleida and then take one of
the Monmantell y Alsina-
Graells buses that provide
daily connections to Andorra.

Located at an altitude of 2,350 m (7,700 ft) at Coma III de Grandvalira, the largest ski slope in the Pyrenees, and offering impressive views of Grau Roig cirque, the Iglú Hotel leaves no visitor indifferent.

While outside snow storms blow and temperatures reach extreme lows, inside the body temperature of the guests manages to maintain a respectable 5 °C. The igloo-rooms, the design of which changes yearly, are lit by the glow of candlelight and provide beds furnished with specialized equipment: sheepskins and feather duvets made for temperatures as low as −40 °C. The Romantic igloos even have two-person sleeping bags.

In addition to weather-appropriate clothing, don't forget to pack your swimwear: two of the igloos have an outdoor jacuzzi (one of which is reserved for the Romantic suite), which lets you observe the stars while relaxing in water at 36 °C.

Built every year in December and the result of more than 2,700 hours of work, the hotel is ephemeral. When spring arrives, it simply melts like snow in the sun.

SUITE WITH ROTATING BED
AT THE YEATMAN HOTEL
Dedicated to the grape

THE YEATMAN HOTEL **15**
Rua do Choupelo
4400-088 Vila Nova de
Gaia (Porto), Portugal
+351 22 013 3100
reservations@
theyeatman.com
www.theyeatman.com

ROOMS AND RATES
Twelve suites and seventy
guest rooms from €215
(breakfast included).
Rate for the main suite
(126 m²) furnished with
a rotating bed: €750.

DIRECTIONS
By car, from the south
(Coimbra/Lisbon/Algarve),
take the A29 or A1 motorway
towards Porto/Ponte
Arrábida. Take the Gaia/
Afurada exit, turn right
towards Afurada and follow
"Cais de Gaia". When you
reach the river, turn right
and, at the roundabout,
take the second exit, where
you'll see a sign indicating
"Caves de Vinho do Porto".
Continue straight ahead.
From the north (Porto,
airport, Viana do Castelo/
Spain), take the A28 or
A3 motorway towards
Lisbon/Ponte Arrábida.
After the Arrábida bridge,
take the first exit towards
Gaia/Afurada then follow
the directions above.
The railway station is just
5 minutes from the hotel.

The Yeatman hotel, opened in late 2010 just a few steps from Porto's historic centre, pays homage to the world of Portuguese wine. While every room is associated with a wine producer, two of them even incorporating massive wooden wine barrels in their decor, the hotel's main suite is truly impressive. Separated from the rest of the building with private direct access to the garden, it is furnished with a rotating bed that lets you admire the logs crackling in the fireplace, the bathroom and, most importantly, the spectacular views of the River Douro and the city of Porto.

The hotel owners, The Fladgate Partnership (which includes the port wine firms Taylor's, Croft and Fonseca), have also added a Caudalie Spa based on vinotherapy: natural ingredients from the vineyards are used in the treatments.

PALACE HOTEL DO BUSSACO

Those who dared cut down a tree were excommunicated!

**PALACE HOTEL
DO BUSSACO** 16
Mata do Bussaco
3050-261 Luso, Portugal
+351 231 937 970
bussaco@almeidahotels.com

ROOMS AND RATES
From €80 for a basic
(double) room to €875
for the royal suite (copy
of the nineteenth-century
apartments of the monarchy).
Sixty-four rooms
including four suites.

DIRECTIONS
Exit 14 on motorway A1
direction Mealhada, between
Porto and Lisbon. The hotel
is located 15 km (9 miles)
ahead, at the heart of the
Bussaco forest. The drive
takes 1 hour from Porto
and 2 hours from Lisbon.

North of Coimbra, in the heart of Bussaco National Forest, stands the Palace Hotel do Bussaco, almost like a mirage. Built in 1885 for the last Portuguese kings, the hotel is a genuine romantic folly inspired by Neuschwanstein Castle, which was built for the Bavarian Ludwig II, a cousin of the King of Portugal.

This sumptuous palace seems to rise out of a fairy tale, as it is surrounded by a mysterious botanic garden dotted with gigantic trees, chapels, monasteries, lakes, belvederes and fountains of crystal-clear water.

It all began in 1628 when Dom João Melo, the count bishop of Coimbra, sent a small group of discalced Carmelite friars to the region to found a place where they could withdraw from the world and build a monastery to devote their lives to prayer and contemplation. The Carmelites also planted many trees, such as the 30 m (100 ft) cedar that has watched the centuries go by since 1644. In 1643, Pope Urban VIII issued a Papal bull to protect these 250 hectares (600 acres) of greenery: anyone who dared cut down a tree would be excommunicated!

The adventure of this Neo-Manueline style hotel began in 1917 when the owner, Alexander de Almeida, restored the abandoned castle and transformed it into a luxury hotel. He kept the original elements relating to the royal family – paintings, frescoes, azulejo panels and furniture – which allow guests to live like royalty for the duration of their stay. The artworks that decorate the hotel are one of the main points of interest for historians and art lovers. On the hotel's walls are rare works illustrating scenes from Portugal's history, such as the Battle of Bussaco, where Wellington defeated Napoleon in 1810, as well as scenes from *The Lusiads*, the epic poem by Portuguese writer Luis de Camões. The azulejos, marvellous sculpted ceilings and stone arches will certainly make a strong impression on art lovers, too.

ITALY
AND REST OF EUROPE

HOTEL RISTORANTE VILLA CRESPI

Une touche de magie

HOTEL RISTORANTE
VILLA CRESPI ❶
Via G. Fava 18
28016 Orta San Giulio
(Novara), Italy
Tel: +39 0322 911902
Fax: +39 0322 911 919
Mobile: +39 334 6052912
www.booking.com/hotel/it/
ristorante-villa-crespi.en.html

ROOMS AND RATES
Fourteen rooms
including eight suites
Rates: from €200 for a double
room, depending on season

Located on the superb Lake Orta, the Villa Crespi is a jewel of Moorish architecture in the heart of the Italian lakes region, about an hour's drive north of Milan. The villa also houses a very reputable restaurant (justly so as it has two Michelin stars) that contributes to the touch of magic you feel when you arrive at this hotel.

The only disadvantages are that the villa isn't directly on the lakefront, contrary to what the hotel's website might suggest. Indeed, a road (and a car park) that can be noisy in high season separates the villa from the lake.

In addition, the rather charming village of Orta isn't as close as you might think – a 15-minute walk away.

Finally, if possible, opt for one of the superb suites as some visitors have been disappointed by the standard rooms.

The villa was built in 1879 for Cristoforo Benigno Crespi, a cotton manufacturer who was so impressed by a trip to Baghdad that he decided to build his own oriental-style palace. In the 1930s, Villa Crespi welcomed King Umberto di Savoia, among other VIPs, and, in the late 1980s, after a time as a spiritual centre, it was converted into a luxury hotel by the current owners.

"WELLBEING" ROOMS AT THE STRAF HOTEL

Massage chair, chromotherapy and aromatherapy in your own room

STRAF HOTEL ❷
Via San Raffaelle 3
20121 Milan, Italy
+39 02 805081
Info@straf.it

ROOMS AND RATES
From €250 (lower
weekend rates)

Located just a few steps from the Duomo, right in the heart of the city, the Straf Hotel is a jewel of raw design.

Of the hotel's sixty-four rooms, twelve are particularly original: the five "Wellbeing" rooms and the seven "Relaxation" rooms.

Although these rooms all share one amenity that is especially pleasant after a long day of work or travel – a massage chair – the "Wellbeing" rooms also offer chromotherapy (therapy by light) and aromatherapy (therapy by scent) systems.

Specifically, once you have chosen an aroma at the reception desk or in your room (a staff member will bring you a selection of essential oils), you turn off the lights, settle into the massage chair, then start the chromotherapy and aromatherapy systems and you're off for half an hour (or more: you can repeat the process indefinitely, although the aromatherapy stops after about 30 minutes) of intense relaxation. The pleasant surprise is that the massage chair is particularly well-programmed and effective – you might even find yourself moaning with pleasure when

the programme reaches the "tapping" massage.

The efficient hotel staff provide a very warm welcome and, to top it all, the hotel bar has the good sense to offer the famous Milan appetizer: for the price of a drink (8 euros for a beer), you can help yourself to a buffet of antipasti, sausages, pasta and rice salads, and more. It's the perfect way to dine on a budget. *The* hotel to visit in Milan.

CABRIOLET SUITE OF THE ALBERETA HOTEL

With your head in the stars

CABRIOLET SUITE OF THE ALBERETA HOTEL ❸
Via Vittorio Emanuele 23
25030 Erbusco (Brescia), Italy
+39 030 7760550
www.albereta.it

ROOMS AND RATES
Cabriolet suite from
€450 per night.

Located in the heart of the Franciacorta wine-producing region, the Albereta Hotel is a very prestigious coaching inn with a particularly astonishing room. The well-named Cabriolet suite offers guests the rare opportunity to open the roof just above the bed, making it possible to sleep in communion with nature.

Indeed, the feeling of falling asleep while watching the stars – literally – or of dozing in the morning to the sound of chirping birds is truly divine.

But you should nevertheless check the weather forecast before leaving the roof open all night long …

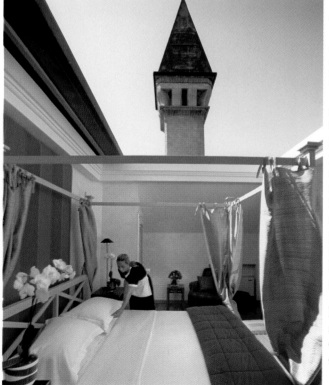

The room also has a small terrace that provides a pretty view of Lake Iseo.

The hotel is also famous for the superb cuisine of Gualtiero Marchesi (two Michelin stars), which you definitely shouldn't miss (the same goes for the little surprise at the beginning of dinner, in the dining room, when a painting disappears into the wall to reveal the kitchens behind a large glass window).

Last but not least, the hotel has a Henri Chenot spa, the reputation of which is firmly established.

HOTEL PARCHI DEL GARDA

"The first 4D avatar hotel with Hollywood-style special effects"

HOTEL PARCHI DEL GARDA ❹
Via Brusa
Pacengo di Lazise
Lake Garda 37017, Italy
+39 345 2307 460
info@hpdg.it
www.hotelparchidelgarda.it

ROOMS AND RATES
4 theme rooms,
from €210 to €250 midweek.
233 in total

This resort property, just 10 minutes from Lake Garda's most famous theme park, offers four theme rooms that include state-of-the-art sensory experiences using animatronic technology under guest control. Currently only four rooms are available:

Aki's cave: enter the hotel mascot's cave together with your children. The fantastic inhabitants of the cave will welcome you in this magic atmosphere, where you can interact with the Spirit of the Lake and other hidden characters through a special keyboard.

Pirates' Galleon room: this representation of a merchant ship creates the atmosphere and charm of the pirates' world, using artificial intelligence robots to interact with guests.

Parco Giardino Sigurtà room: set in nature, with green meadows, flowers blooming in the morning and tree trunks. Special effects give guests a fantastic stay in this virtual Parco Giardino Sigurtà through "Show Control" technology.

Natura Viva room: to live the experience of a photographer on African safari, with a very peculiar setting: a bed built on a tree dominates the scene and guests can look for the animals hidden among the trees using special software.

BYBLOS ART HOTEL

An extravagant hotel

BYBLOS ART HOTEL **5**
Via Cedrare 78
37029 Corrubbio di
Negarine (Verona), Italy
+39 045 6855555
www.byblosarthotel.com

ROOMS AND RATES
From 250 euros per night

Just a 20-minute drive from Verona, the Byblos Art Hotel is spectacular and entirely dedicated to contemporary art. You'll find masterpieces throughout the grandiose architecture of this typically Italian villa.

In the rooms, as in the public areas, you'll be surprised by over a hundred works of art by fifty different artists that clash with the traditional atmosphere, thus creating a rather eccentric ambiance that might remind some guests of the *Alice in Wonderland* film.

Although the effect may seem a bit garish, the hotel is nevertheless as near as you get to a museum of contemporary art so is definitely worth a visit.

TORRE PRENDIPARTE

A cosy tower for two

TORRE PRENDIPARTE ❻
Via Sant'Alò 7
Bologna 40126, Italy
+39 335 5616858
info@prendiparte.it
www.prendiparte.it

ROOMS AND RATES
Single suite for two from
€250 to €300 per night.

Matteo Giovanardi has turned his former home – the second-highest of Bologna's famous medieval towers – into a one-bedroom romantic hideaway. Following extensive restoration, all twelve floors of this twelfth-century tower, standing 65 m (213 ft) high, are accessible, including a roof terrace offering breathtaking views across the Old Town. Even the original wall graffiti of the prison cells at the foot of the tower has been preserved!

The main living and sleeping area, lounge, etc., are housed on the second and third floors, in an elegant old-world space with vaulted ceilings, furnished with family heirlooms. Above this is a kitchen, where guests fix themselves a self-service breakfast, and a dining room where candlelit dinners can be arranged —accompanied, should you so desire, by a string quartet or medieval-style minstrels.

TREEHOUSES AT LA PIANTATA

The largest treehouses in Europe

AGRITURISMO LA PIANTATA ❼
Loc. La Piantata
Strada Provinciale
113 Arlenese s/n
01010 Arlena di
Castro (VT), Italy
www.lapiantata.it
+39 333 371 0828 or
+39 335 604 9630

ROOMS AND RATES
€330 or €390 per night,
breakfast included.

At the heart of their estate La Piantata, which lies between Tuscany and Umbria, Rosella and Renzo Stucchi have had the two largest treehouses in Europe built at a height of 7 m and 8 m (23–26 ft) above ground. The 44 m² treehouse is charming and discreetly luxurious, while the 87 m² one is in a more high-tech style.

According to their designer, Alain Laurens of the "Cabane perchée" team, these treehouses are among the most beautiful he has ever built.

Although both treehouses lie in the middle of 12 hectares (30 acres) of organic lavender, we prefer the smaller one for its more natural feel. It is also more isolated from the rest of the estate.

Treehouse guests also have access to the estate's swimming pool. Seven other rooms and apartments are also available.

MASSERIA CERVAROLO

Sixteenth-century farmstead with restored trulli dwellings

MASSERIA CERVAROLO ❽
C. da Cervarolo snc
Ostuni 72017
Puglia, Italy
+39 831 303729
info@masseriacervarolo.it
www.masseriacervarolo.it

ROOMS AND RATES
Seventeen rooms,
three in *trulli*
Double rooms from
€145 to €295
A minimum stay applies
during high season.

LOCATION
Masseria Cervarolo is located
between the airports of
Bari (50 min) and Brindisi
(30 min) where you can
easily hire a car. You're based
in La Valle d'Itria – the very
heart of Puglia. With the
beaches of the Adriatic 12 km
(7.5 miles) away and two
large nature reserves close
by (Fiume Morelli – 15 min;
Torre Guaceto – 25 min),
there is plenty of opportunity
for walking or resting on the
beach, cooled by sea breezes.

This splendid *masseria* (manor farm) dating from the sixteenth century creates a warm sensation of peace. It is based around six ancient *trulli* – conical stone dwellings built without mortar so that they could be taken down should conditions require. These were the original DIY properties of their time and have been lovingly restored and connected to the main building to provide three of the seventeen bedrooms.

The main property was once a working farm, presided over by noble families. Brought back to its original splendour, it is furnished with antiques and original fabrics.

ATELIER SUL MARE

Hotel-museum of modern art

ATELIER SUL MARE 9
Via Cesare Battisti, 4
Castel di Tusa (Me)
Sicily - Italy
+39 921 334 295
+39 921 334 283
E-mail: ateliersulmare@
interfree.it
www.ateliersulmare.it

ROOMS AND RATES
Forty rooms -
Thirteen art rooms.
Located halfway between
Palermo and Messina
Thirteen art rooms from
€70 to €145 per person.

The creation of Antonio Presti, who is quite a character, Atelier sul Mare is more than a hotel. Located halfway between Palermo and Messina, it's well worth a trip even if it's not the height of luxury.

When planning your trip, don't rely on the hotel website, which doesn't do justice to the place. Although the road you can see between the hotel and the beach does exist, it turns into a cul-de-sac after a short distance and is little used. On the other hand, the view is sublime: the water comes almost up to the windows and the Aeolian Islands form a magnificent and mysterious background.

The tone of the hotel is set at the entrance: Atelier sul Mare is totally given over to modern art. In contrast to many establishments calling themselves art hotels, here the word "art" is not taken in vain: each room has actually been designed by a different artist.

Of the forty rooms in the hotel, thirteen have been designed by modern artists. We particularly recommend the "Prophet's Room", in homage to Pier Paolo Pasolini (by Dario Bellezza, Adele Cambria, Antonio Presti), "Trinacria" (by Maurizio Staccioli) with its immense triangular bed, and "Sigismond's Tower" (by Raoul Ruiz), in which the roof can be opened manually to let you sleep under the stars, spread-eagled on a vast round bed installed in the depths of a cylinder.

It should also be noted that Antonio Presti, in accordance with his social conscience, wanted to give the place a democratic character and make it accessible to the less well-off. So he has deliberately kept prices low (from €70 per person per night) and it's not unknown for him to offer one or two nights' hospitality to passing artists.

ANTONIO PRESTI

The son of a wealthy Sicilian cement manufacturer, Antonio Presti soon took a different direction and found his niche as troublemaker of the Sicilian art scene. Although threatened several times by the Mafia, Antonio has always held his own, claiming to want to "terrorize the terrorists". Today, thanks to his success and subsequent publicity, he's left alone and can concentrate on his main goal: the democratization of art.

His first major project was at Catania in eastern Sicily: to help the residents of the dreary suburbs of the town see the relevance of art to their own lives, he had the bright idea of having giant portraits made of local residents by world-famous photographers. These images were later hung directly on the façades of Catania social housing blocks and let residents gradually discover a certain sense of self-pride. In contrast to many projects of this nature, Antonio wanted at all costs to avoid the typical syndrome of modern art being brought to working-class suburbs and then, misunderstood by most people as something far removed from their own experience, taken away again, leaving behind little trace of its passage. Here, the residents truly feel at home with their art all around them.

After Atelier sul Mare, Antonio is now working on a new iconoclastic project: in a bid to draw attention to the impending ecological crisis in the river near Palermo station, with support in the media from Danielle Mitterrand, wife of the former French president, he brought along hundreds of children who symbolically poured into the river fresh water taken from the source upstream... Antonio now plans to install sculptures on the site, and as he says, these may be the first modern artworks ever to be displayed in an open sewer.

ITALIE

KAROSTAS CIETUMS
The only military prison in Europe open to tourists

KAROSTAS CIETUMS ⑩
Invalīdu Street 4
Karosta
Liepāja LV-3402, Latvia
+ 371 263 69 470
info@karostascietums.lv
www.karostascietums.lv

ROOMS AND RATES
Facilities are basic and you can sign up for experiences where you'll discover some of the harsh treatments experienced by prisoners. Beds are hard and blankets thin. To ensure that all participants are aware of, and willing to comply with, the treatment they'll receive, they are required to sign a special agreement in advance. From 10 Latvian lati per night. Other tours are additionally available, including the opportunity to take a guided tour of the north forts and see underground labyrinths by torchlight.

LOCATION
On the western coast of Latvia, around 175 km (110 miles) from Riga.

In 1890 a military base north of Liepaja was constructed following orders from Russian tsar Alexander III. His son, tsar Nicholas II, named the new base "Port of Alexander III" however following Latvian independence in 1918 it assumed the title of "Kara Osta" (War Port). The port was strategically important as it was ice-free throughout the year and grew in importance, with ship and submarine refitting workshops and dockyard facilities. The growing population needed a naval port prison or guardhouse. The building was erected about 1900 and until 1997 this was where military personnel served their terms for breach of discipline. With powers changing, its prisoners changed as well – and inmates included revolutionaries, seamen and non-commissioned officers of the tsarist army, deserters from the German Wehrmacht, enemies of the people in Stalin's time, soldiers of both the Soviet and the Latvian army, and other rebels. Now closed, the prison lets visitors experience the harsh life of detainees in a variety of ways for groups and individual guests. From a short overnight tour to themed activities for groups, the prison hosts a variety of events based on recorded history and experiences.

BLOW UP HALL ⁵⁰⁵⁰

Electronic art hotel in a former brewery

BLOWUPHALL⁵⁰⁵⁰ ⓫
ul. Kościuszki 42
61-891 Poznań, Poland
+48 61 657 99 80
blowup@
blowuphall5050.com
www.blowuphall5050.com

ROOMS AND RATES
22 rooms from 880 Zloty
(€200) to 1400 Zloty (€330)
per room, per night.

LOCATION
Midway between Berlin and
Warsaw, the hotel is less than
10 minutes' walk from the
Old Market Square, which is
a lively area offering a wide
selection of bars, restaurants
and cafés next to the
sixteenth-century city hall.
The hotel is 10 minutes from
the central railway station
and around 20 minutes drive
from low-cost airline served
Poznań Lawica airport.

No central reception area. No room key. A black-faced lift, taking you to a black corridor with black doors. No room numbers. Clicking a button on the iPhone offered for use during your stay lights a screen next to your room – and the door opens.

Welcome to the monochrome world of Blow Up Hall ⁵⁰⁵⁰ in the former Stary Browar (brewery).

Taking styling cues from 1966 cult movie *Blow-Up*, the brewery was transformed under the guidance of Polish businesswoman and art collector Grażyna Kulczyk and Mexican-Canadian electronic artist Rafael Lozano Hemmer into a combination of stylish shopping arcade, contemporary dance centre and art-themed hotel. The 5050 notation reflects the philosophical foundation of all Kulczyk's ventures – where art is the 50% core, with the remainder a complementary element – in the case of the hotel, pleasure.

Modern art adorns the walls, including a Lozano-Hemmer interactive centrepiece, which takes video images, replaying them as pixilated images on a giant screen.

The hotel bar and restaurant are understandably considered a trendy focal point for locals and residents alike.

HOTEL JEŠTĚD

Amazing view in award-winning architectural design

Hotel Ještěd ⑫
Horní Hanychov
153460 08 Liberec,
Czech Republic
+485 104 291
recepce@jested.cz
www.jested.cz

Rooms and rates
Two suites and twelve
double rooms.
The hotel facilities are
three-star standard and
offer two suites and twelve
double rooms, extended
with a further five rooms of
a lower one-star category.
Double rooms cost from
CZK1,660 (Czech koruna)
and CZK3,400 for suites.
Double rooms are more
expensive on Friday, Saturday
and Bank Holidays.

Location
The hotel is reached by cable
car from nearby Liberec –
capital of the Nisa region.

From the middle of the nineteenth century Ještěd has welcomed walkers with a refreshment stop, however when the lookout tower caught fire in 1963 the opportunity to build something more spectacular was recognized. For three years designs were considered on the theme of a TV transmission tower, separate restaurant with small hotel. However, architect Karel Hubáček entered with a radical design that combined all these, to universal acclaim. The mountain-top location demanded the use of new construction methods and materials as the TV transmitter antennas needed to be enclosed within the structure to cope with the severe climatic conditions.

In 1969, the architectural solution was awarded the world-renowned Perret Prize, and in 2000 it was awarded the title of Best Czech Building of the twentieth century.

The Hundred Competition

The most peculiar event organized in connection with Ještěd was The Hundred Competition. The participant's only and simple goal was, in the shortest possible time, to ascend a hundred times to the top of the mountain. Tourists took the competition very seriously and it has recently been revived. Serious competitors have ascended the mountain multiple times a day, with a record of twelve trips in a single day by Rudolf Kaushka in 1922, and during 1937 Lilly Flassak made an ascent 709 times. Competitors are celebrated with their own beer glass with name and the number of ascents or badges celebrating their achievements. These are kept in the bar of Hotel Ještěd hotel.

MEDIEVAL HOTEL DĚTENICE

Themed hotel providing medieval experiences in an authentic setting

MEDIEVAL HOTEL DĚTENICE ⑬
507 24 Dětenice
Bohemia, Czech Republic
+493 599 161
stredovekyhotel@detenice.cz
www.detenice.cz

ROOMS AND RATES
41 themed rooms from
€130 - €180 for a single night
package on a half board basis.

This property is a fantastic escape from day-to-day boredom and way better than any chain hotel for stories to tell your friends. Guests can step back to a more rustic time and enjoy the authentic and imaginative attention to detail: providing entertainment, honest food, wine, beer and the whole atmosphere to make your trip memorable and truly MEDIEVAL!

Guests are welcomed by a beggar or a witch at the hotel reception desk and might even be shown to their room by a dwarf with a lantern. While the reception area has a straw-strewn floor with a medieval stove with open fire, don't think that you'll be uncomfortable here. The candle-lit rooms have wooden floors, simple rustic furniture and unique bathrooms that look like rough latrines, but actually hide modern flush toilets and showers behind the rough hewn-timber facings. Throughout the hotel you'll find that underneath the decor, the facilities and service are modern.

Dinner is served in the Brewery Tavern next door – an extravaganza of banqueting, drinking and regular live entertainment medieval style. Feast on food prepared on a traditional open fire and beer served by tough-but-tender wenches of the inn. Be entertained by swordsmen, jugglers and dancers in the candle-lit vaults.

After a night of revelry in the tavern and enjoying the night bar, you'll be ready for the medieval breakfast, too!

HOSTEL CELICA

Former prison transformed into funky art house hostel

Hostel Celica ⑭
Metelkova 8
SI – 1000 Ljubljana
Slovenia
+ 386 1 230 97 00
www.hostelcelica.com

ROOMS AND RATES
Twenty cells plus
dormitory, suites and
disabled access room.
There are a total of twenty-
nine rooms, including suites
and dormitories in the attic
space and a room with
disabled access on the ground
floor. Some of the twenty cell
rooms are for two occupants,
and others have three beds.
Prices for two-bed cells are
from €23 in low season, and
three-bed cells from €18,
all per person per night.
Guests are additionally
required to pay a nightly
sales tax of €1.01 per person.
There are minimum-stay
requirements at peak
periods and a single-
occupancy supplement.

Following the departure of the Yugoslav army in 1991, it took until July 2003 for this former prison to be turned into the hostel and art centre complex that greets visitors today. Due to the slow bureaucracy of the former Yugoslavia, transferring ownership of these former army barracks from government ministries to the peoples' collective set up to run the hostel by the city of Ljubljana was a surprisingly lengthy undertaking. However, the patience and tenacity of the artists who have supported this project has finally been repaid with a well-admired conversion to a 'funky, hip' hostel that is the recipient of many accolades for the cell rooms and overall hospitality.

There are twenty cell rooms on the first floor, each decorated by a different artist. Some have added mezzanine bunk beds to use the small room space efficiently and most have retained the prison window bars for an authentic confinement feel. None of the cells are en suite, however the toilets upstairs are clean and functional, if not a little busy in the mornings.

The attic space has apartments with en suite facilities, but they aren't in the cell style and may get noisy if there's a band playing in the café. Live music is usually on Tuesdays, and the hostel bar serves keenly priced beer that helps to attract a friendly artist and commune subculture which is lively until late at night – or early in the morning at weekends. Pack earplugs if you're a light sleeper, or if your room is near the café.

Breakfast is provided in a glass-covered terrace, as is a much in-demand internet link that can be provided in cells for an additional charge. The restaurant is open for light snacks during the day, but with the centre of town only 10 minutes' walk away, most guests eat out at the many local cafés and restaurants at some time during their stay.

LIGHTHOUSES ALONG THE CROATIAN COAST

Sleep in a lighthouse in Croatia

ELEVEN LIGHTHOUSES ALONG
THE CROATIAN COAST **⑮**
www.plovput.hr/eng

ROOMS AND RATES
€80–€150 a night for
four people, depending
on the lighthouse
Payment by transfer in
advance. Given the high cost
of bank transfers to Croatia,
we suggest paying the full
price in one payment.
Transport by boat
not included.

Lighthouses located
on islands:
Sv. Ivan na pučini
(Note: there's no real beach
despite what is mentioned
on the Plovput website)
Porer
Prišnjak
Pločica
Palagruža
Sveti Andrija
Host

In the 1990s, Croatia began offering lodgings in eleven lighthouses located along the Croatian coastline.

The unique fact about these lighthouses is that they are still in use. If a lighthouse keeper still holds a position there (which is most often the case – you can check on the website), then for a few days you can fulfil your dream and share his lighthouse-keeping experience. For a small additional sum (as they are not obliged to do so), most keepers will take you on a tour of the lighthouse and up to the very top.

You should note that guests don't sleep in the lighthouse itself, but in the attached buildings.

Spending a few days in a working lighthouse is a unique experience. To accentuate the magic of the moment, we strongly suggest choosing one of the seven lighthouses (listed here) that are actually located on remote islands, far from civilization.

The downside is that this Robinson Crusoe-like experience might not please everyone. The islands are often rather arid (no vegetation) and weren't necessarily chosen for tourism but rather for their coastal location. Consequently, there are rarely any true beaches and the currents around the islands are often quite strong. Also, as the islands are rather small, it is inadvisable to moor boats there, as the sea is usually too rough. The keepers often have to use a small crane to hoist their boats out of the water. So it can be very difficult to hire a boat to explore the surrounding areas, which means you'll be rather isolated on the island.

Yet for those who are looking for this isolation, the experience is fantastic and children love it.

Note that there are no shops on site. You should do all your shopping beforehand.

BABY GRAND HOTEL

A touch of New York in Greece

BABY GRAND HOTEL **⑯**
65 Athinas & Lycourgou street
GR 105 51 Athens, Greece
+30 210 325 0900
bg@classicalhotels.com
www.babygrandhotel.com

ROOMS AND RATES
76 graffiti rooms and suites
Standard graffiti rooms
are around €105–€130
per room, inclusive of
taxes, and breakfast.
Suites from €150.

LOCATION
Across from Kotzia Square,
the hotel is a 15 minute
walk from the Athens
Archaeological Museum and
close to the metro station
on line 2 of Omonia Station.
With a location so easily
served by the modern buses
and metro lines created
for the 2004 Olympics,
you're within easy reach of
all the traditional Athens
sights, from the Acropolis
and its museum (using
the new Acropolis metro
stop), to the Parthenon.
The hotel is near the
revitalized downtown area
of Athens, where you'll
find the newly restored
nineteenth-century Athens
Market with its colourful
stalls and craft shops.

From the moment you view the first-floor reception desks of reclaimed Mini Cooper cars, you realize that the Baby Grand team have invested in a more quirky and funky appeal. Graffiti theme rooms are decorated by different Greek artists, giving each a completely different feel – from legendary cartoon characters to Japanese art, fairytale landscapes, street art, flowers and dreaming creatures. Some might recoil at the plastic vines and make-believe fantasy in a classical setting – but the fun and frivolity soon overcome any misgivings, as underneath the art you'll find quality furnishings, marble bathrooms and top service.

DENMARK

NORTH
SEA

BALTIC
SEA

Flensburg

Kiel

Stralsund

Rostock

Lübeck

Schwerin

Wilhelmshaven

Hamburg

Schwerin

Szczecin

POLAND

Bremerhaven

Bremen

NETHERLANDS

Oldenburg

Bremen

Hannover

Wolfsburg

BERLIN **1 - 4**

Potsdam

Frankfurt

Poznan →

Utrecht

Osnabrück

Braunschweig

Magdeburg

Hildesheim

Münster

Bielefeld

Paderborn

Dessau

Halle

Leipzig

Cottbus

Wroclaw →

Essen

Dortmund

Kassel

Göttingen

Hamm

6 Wroclaw

Duisburg

Siegen

Erfurt

Jena

Gera

Dresden

Düsseldorf

Wuppertal

Köln

Aachen

Bonn

Chemnitz

Zwickau

BELGIUM

Koblenz

Wiesbaden

Frankfurt

GERMANY

CZECH
REPUBLIC

LUXEMBOURG

Mainz

Darmstadt

Würzburg

Bamberg

Bayreuth

Trier

Ludwigshafen

Kaiserslautern

Mannheim
Heidelberg

Nürnberg

Saarbrücken

Heilbronn

Karlsruhe
Pforzheim

Stuttgart

Regensburg

Passau

Zwettl

Krems

Stockerau

FRANCE

5 Reutlingen

Ingolstadt

Ulm

Augsburg

München

Sankt Pölten

WIEN

Freiburg

Salzburg

Linz

Wels

7 **10**

Eisenstac

Wiener
Neustadt

Schaffhausen

Winterthur

Sankt Gallen

Bregenz

Saalfelden

AUSTRIA

Graz

9

Basel

Zürich

Innsbruck

8

Biel

Luzern

12 **15**

St. Anton

Neuchâtel

16

Bern

SWITZERLAND

Freiburg

Interlaken

Spittal

11

Klagenfurt

Maribor

Lausanne

13

SLOVENIA

Geneva

14

Lugano

CROATI

ITALY

ADRIATIC
SEA

0   50   100 km

GERMANY, AUSTRIA AND SWITZERLAND

OSTEL HOSTEL

60s and 70s GDR German retro

OSTEL HOSTEL BERLIN ❶
Wriezener Karee 5
10243 Berlin, Germany
+49 30 25 768660
contact@ostel.eu
www.ostel.eu

ROOMS AND RATES
From €15 to €120
per night per person

LOCATION
The hotel is located in the up
and coming Friedrichshain
district. You're 250 m from
the Ostbahnhof station where
you can connect with the
ICE and regional trains.

One of the casualties of German reunification was the demolition of many of the former East German *Plattenbauwohnung* tower blocks – a kind of mass-produced concrete apartment building that came to symbolize life in the communist bloc. A couple of former circus performers have used the resurgence in retro chic to rescue communist-era furnishings to decorate this property in the style of the period.

Sitting on a plastic chair in a room, overlooked by a portrait of former GDR leader Erich Honecker, surrounded by stunning 70s wallpaper and too much brown fabric won't appeal to everyone, but this is certainly a cost effective and quirky place to stay in Berlin.

PROPELLER ISLAND CITY LODGE

Outrageous bedroom designs from upside-down to inside a coffin

**PROPELLER ISLAND
CITY LODGE** ❷
Allbrecht Achilles Strasse 58
10709 Berlin
Germany
+49 30 891 9016
www.propellerisland.de

ROOMS AND RATES
Thirty-one outrageous rooms.
From €69 to €190 per night.
Breakfast is €7 per person.

LOCATION
You're 25 minutes by bus
from the central Tegel
airport, or 45 minutes
from the larger Schonefeld.
The nearest U-Bahn stop is
Adenauer Platz, a 10 minute
walk from the hotel.

From an upside-down room with a bed on the ceiling, to coffin and prison-cell rooms, this is no ordinary designer hotel. Originally created to pay for the musical interests of artist Lars Stroschen, the hotel grew from a couple of rented rooms to today's thirty-one individually designed rooms.

Some rooms are minimalist in their decoration – "Therapy" is completely white, with a variety of room colouring made possible using a series of coloured lights. The big mirror above the bed allows you to literally see yourself in a different light.

Other rooms offer an increasingly surreal experience, with the "Gruft / Coffin" offering a pair of coffins for beds, and "Freedom" a recreation of a prison cell, complete with escape through the wall. "Upside-Down" has a bed, table and furnishings suspended from the ceiling – and you sleep by opening a loft hatch in the floor. Not recommended after a night enjoying the many bars of Berlin!

The "Mirror" room completely surrounds you with mirrors as you'd expect, but taken to such extremes that it provides a kaleidoscope experience from every angle. Some rooms demonstrate the sense of humour of the artist, such as "Space-Cube" where a divider can be lowered to turn the double bed into two singles, perhaps after a late-night argument! Equally bizarre is the "Padded Cell".

Lars has not only built the rooms but the team that support guests from scratch – and everywhere you look you can see a creative genius at work. While there is no restaurant, you're in central Berlin so won't struggle to find a choice of food.

Once you've tried one room, you'll want to sample them all.

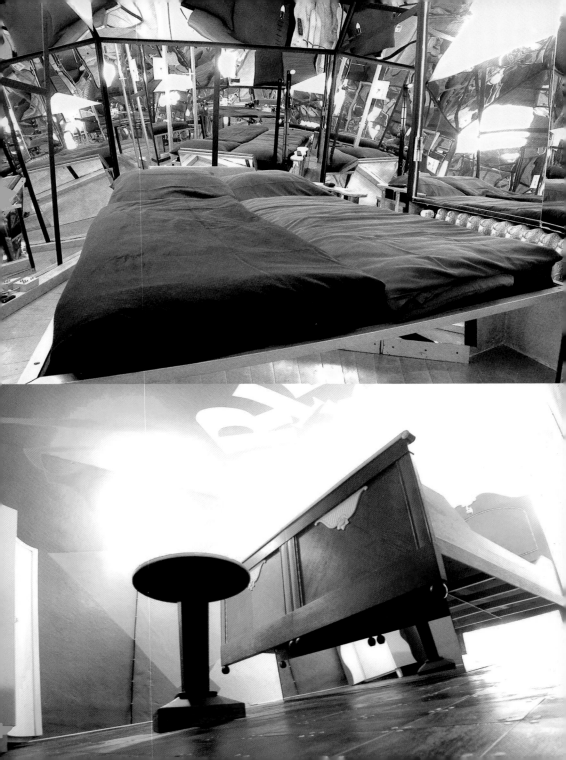

MICHELBERGER HOTEL

The first hotel in space

MICHELBERGER HOTEL ❸
Warschauer Strasse 39/40
10243 Berlin, Germany
+49 302 977 859-0
reservations@
michelbergerhotel.com
www.michelbergerhotel.com

ROOMS AND RATES
119 rooms
Double rooms from €59

Opened in 2009 in an old factory in the trendy Friedrichshain neighbourhood, this hotel created by Tom Michelberger, who gave the site his name, is marvellously characteristic of Berlin: casual, creative, sexy and surprising.

Thanks to the site's original structure, architect Werner Aisslinger was able to design rooms with impressively high ceilings. It was then time for Anja Knamer to go to town: salvaged lamps, books in metal cages, and more.

A truly stimulating place.

KÜNSTLERHEIM LUISE

Co-operative art gallery where you can spend the night

ARTE LUISE KUNSTHOTEL ❹
Luisenstrasse 19,
10117 Berlin
Germany
+49 30 28448 0
info@luise-berlin.com
www.luise-berlin.com

ROOMS AND RATES
Fifty en suite rooms.
Doubles from €121–150 per
room per night according
to season and availability,
inclusive of local sales taxes.

LOCATION
The Arte Luise is situated
in the heart of this vibrant
city, close by the Tiergarten
park and Spree River, within
view of the Reichstag
building, Friedrichstrasse,
Unter den Linden and
the Brandenburg Gate.

Guests walking into a room at the Künstlerheim Luise art hotel find themselves within a work of art where every one of the fifty rooms is unique – even more so when you appreciate the partnership that the hotel makes with the artists who have decorated every room. A percentage of the profit from the individually created rooms is provided as payment – plus a number of free overnight stays. So while the art is stunning the rooms remain functional and all rooms and suites have a shower or bath, TV and free wireless internet.

The building itself is a residential palace dating from 1825, which like so many old properties in the former GDR had fallen into disrepair. The efforts of an enterprising group of young artists in 1984 transformed the property from a dilapidated art studio into a boutique hotel. In 2003, an annex was added to enclose the courtyard. This addition, as well as overall refurbishment and fitting of double glazing, has at last blocked the noise of the nearby elevated S-Bahn. Previously, earplugs were a necessary addition to guests' nightwear. While the classical style of the main building has been maintained, the new addition is more in tune with urban art, using exposed concrete, steel and glass. This serves to highlight the artistic nature of the different rooms and provides a gallery space for regular exhibitions next to the lobby.

As well as rooms and gallery space there is a restaurant, "Habel", named after the old vintner of Frederick the Great, and founder of the Berlin winery Gebrüder Habel in 1779.

V8 HOTEL

Zeppelin airfield buildings converted to a motor-themed hotel

V8 Hotel ❺
Graf-Zeppelin-Platz
71034 Böblingen, Germany
+49 7031 306 9880
info@v8hotel.de
www.v8hotel.de

Rooms and rates
Thirty-four motor-
themed rooms
Rates are from €145 for
double rooms, €165 for
theme rooms and the
Zeppelin suite €450.

Location
The hotel is a 5 minute walk
from Böblingen S-Bahn rail
station on line S1, which
connects to the S2 and S3
lines if you're visiting one
of the many trade shows
in Sindelfingen or arriving
at Stuttgart airport.
If driving, from the A81
take exit 23 Böblingen
/ Sindelfingen and at
the first traffic light turn
right in the direction of
Böblingen. Then turn right
onto Graf-Zeppelin-Platz.
Hotel V8 Meilenwerk
Stuttgart is on your left.

The four-star rated V8 Hotel is part of the Meilenwerk complex on the old Zeppelin airfield near Böblingen. Partnered by the Porsche Museum and Mercedes Benz, car enthusiasts, collectors and restoration specialists gather together to enjoy heritage motor vehicles on display in the Legend Hall of the main event building. Collectors of classic cars may even park their car in glass viewing boxes, so that others can see the repair and servicing taking place.

The V8 Hotel itself occupies the original Bauhaus-style (1928) airport hotel building, now completely restored and updated as a listed building in its own right.

The standard rooms have some great wall photography but the theme rooms really take the automotive element to a new level. Perhaps you wish for the luxury of sleeping in a converted white Mercedes bed – bright and polished from the carwash? Maybe airbrushed custom paintwork and chrome is more your style in the Tuning bedroom? Or the 53 Beetle Herbie parked up as a bed in the Petrol Station room?

A Cadillac bed and artwork themed around the drive-in cinemas of the 50s and 60s, or a room themed for the outdoors, in V8 Camp?

While everyone will have a favourite, the Morris Minor car bed in the Workshop room – complete with mechanic under the car, deserves special mention. Your bed is hoisted on lifting jacks, and your bedside table is a drum of oil. A mechanic's workbench is your writing desk.

BAUMHAUS HOTEL

First treehouse hotel to open in Germany

Baumhaus Hotel ❻
Fa. Künstlerische
Holzgestaltung
Jürgen Bergmann
02829 Neisseaue
OT Zentendorf
Görlitz - Germany
+49 35891 491 0
Info@kulturinsel.de
www.kulturinsel.de

Rooms and rates
Five treehouses for up
to four guests each.
From €180 to €220 for up
to four people, including
breakfast and tax. Check out
their last-minute deals as
well, which offer up to 27%
discounts for bookings with
less than four days' notice.

Location
By car, leave the A4
(Dresden-Bautzen-Görlitz)
autobahn at Görlitz, towards
Rothenburg. Around 2 km
(1 mile) from Zentendorf
you'll see signs to the site.

First opened in June 2005, it is arguable whether this is the first treehouse hotel in Germany or the craziest.

Whatever the decision, these two-storey dwellings are furnished in a rustic style, with brightly coloured walls and off-angle windows, and are sure to entertain.

Each treehouse contains an "emergency toilet", but if only for the sake of the cleaners, a central toilet block is provided on one of the lower decks, with running water.

The central area also contains a particularly German addition – a mini-bar filled with beer ready for evening guest celebrations.

Treehouses additionally share an extraordinary open-air, chilled-water shower with a metal grid floor, so you can see the ground below you. Whether this is for health reasons, for waking up, or perhaps because of the provision of the guest mini-bar, sobering up is unknown.

Some treehouses have small balconies and each is themed according to the regional tradition and myths of trolls and fairy folk.

Electric heating is provided for those brave enough to extend the summer open season into November and risk snow.

A breakfast buffet is served in the main site restaurant.

PIXEL HOTEL

Collective of five unconventional rooms in unused premises

PIXEL HOTEL ❼
Altstadt 28
4020 Linz, Austria
+43650 743 79 53
office@pixelhotel.at
www.pixelhotel.at

ROOMS AND RATES
The five rooms all have a
king-size bed, bathroom
with shower, WC, minibar,
TV and Wi-Fi. Some also
include the use of two
bicycles. Single occupancy
is from €107 and couples
pay from €124 inclusive
of breakfast vouchers.

A project for the Linz 2009 European Capital of Culture created a hotel where creatively designed rooms are dispersed across the city. *Pixel im Hof* provides a 1960s camping caravan, installed inside an industrial warehouse. *Pixel mit Garten* is a flat and shopfront converted to showcase an indoor garden with attached bedroom. *Pixel in der Textilpassage* provides a living space on four separate levels, dominated by a floating island where you'll find your bed for the night. It also includes the Neverland den, conceived with a ceiling too low for adults and filled instead with kids' toys and pillows. *Pixel in der Volksküche* includes a remote-controlled foldaway bed in the building that is home to Architekturforum Oberösterreich – itself a showcase of modernist, minimal decoration. *Pixel am Wasser* provides a room on a 1958 tug, MSZ *Traisen*, now restored and lying at anchor in Linz harbour.

All over Linz, these unconventional but unused premises have been converted into hotel-style rooms. They're in a mixture of residential areas, downtown, industrial zones and working-class neighbourhoods – and guests will find different experiences in each.

The features and conveniences of a modern hotel room are maintained: double bed, living area, bathroom, minibar, Wi-Fi, TV and maid service. For breakfast, guests are provided with vouchers to nearby cafés. Local restaurants serve as the hotel's dining room and pubs with their character and local colour more than make up for the absence of a hotel bar.

SCHNEEDORF

Igloo hotel comfort, in the middle of a ski resort

SCHNEEDORF GMBH ❽
Dorfstraße 7
6432 Sautens
Ötztal / Hochötz, Austria
+43 5252 20157
info@schneedorf.com
www.schneedorf.com

ROOMS AND RATES
Eighteen igloos
Overnight accommodation in
Classic igloos for four people
is €109 per person including
dinner of cheese fondue,
continental buffet breakfast
and sleeping bag rental.
Romantic igloos cost €299
per couple including
champagne, cheese fondue
and breakfast. You also
get the use of double-bed
sleeping bags too!

LOCATION
The Snow Village is situated
in the ski resort of Hochötz
/ Ochsengarten, more than
2,020 m (6,620 ft) above
sea level, close to Sölden
in the Ötztal valley.

Spend the night in Austria's first igloo village, amidst a fantastic mountain panorama in one of the eighteen Classic or Romantic two- and four-person igloos. The Schneedorf offers a mix of unforgettable impressions and activities to enjoy the starry winter sky after the lifts have shut. From the usual winter sport activities such as skiing, snowshoe hiking, snowboarding or toboggan, at the Schneedorf you can also have a relaxing, luxurious time in their mountain sauna — made from local Zirbenwood. At night, nestle down in a fantastic warm expedition sleeping bag, cuddling on the sheepskin, or having champagne with your partner in one of the individual created and carved Romantic igloos.

People often ask if igloos are cold overnight … and the answer is "not really" although the most common problem is that visitors wear too many clothes in their sleeping bags — perspire, and then wake up chilly. Together with the sculpture-decorated main igloo with space for more than sixty people, the snowbar and a separate lounge area, the Schneedorf is perfectly suited for weddings, events and parties.

ROGNER BAD BLUMAU

Spa hotel designed by eccentric Austrian artist Hundertwasser,
with grass-covered roofs and rainbow façades

ROGNER BAD BLUMAU ❾
A 8283 Bad Blumau 100
Austria
+43 3383 5100-0
spa.blumau@rogner.com
www.blumau.com

ROOMS AND RATES

312 designer rooms including eight underground "Forest" houses and thirteen "Eyelid" apartments. Double room prices vary according to season and are from €120 per person per night plus tax, including unlimited use of the spa pool facilities. Suites are additionally available from €260 per night with spa treatment packages available on request.

LOCATION

The hotel is around 56 km (35 miles) from Graz airport and 1 km (1/2 mile) from Bad Blumau railway station for visitors travelling by train.

Inaugurated in 2000, Rogner Bad Blumau has a simply amazing eclectic design with the grass-covered roof of the main buildings following the profile of the rolling hills.

Some of the rooms are underground, with windows facing lit courtyards, while others follow the rolling landscape. A spa is at the centre of the complex, with an award-winning gourmet restaurant among the facilities. The spa has a variety of saunas and health facilities and offers a number of wellness programmes. The hot springs also provide heat and generate power for the resort.

Although the rooms are in differently themed areas, they provide a similar level of guest comfort, room service and en suite facilities. Inside, you could easily be in a well furnished four-star hotel. Outside, however, the story is dramatically different and the views are more in keeping with how you expect a hotel will look on the moon, or in a fantasy world – such is the patchwork of coloured tiles, grass and oddly positioned windows in the overall design.

Hundertwasser's artistic vision shares common themes, bright colours, organic forms, strong individualism, and a rejection of the straight line. Calling straight lines "the devil's tools", his architectural work is comparable to

Antoni Gaudí. His work has been used for flags, stamps, coins, posters, schools, churches and, most impressively, a public toilet in his adopted home of New Zealand; no matter where he went in the world, his watch was always set to New Zealand time.

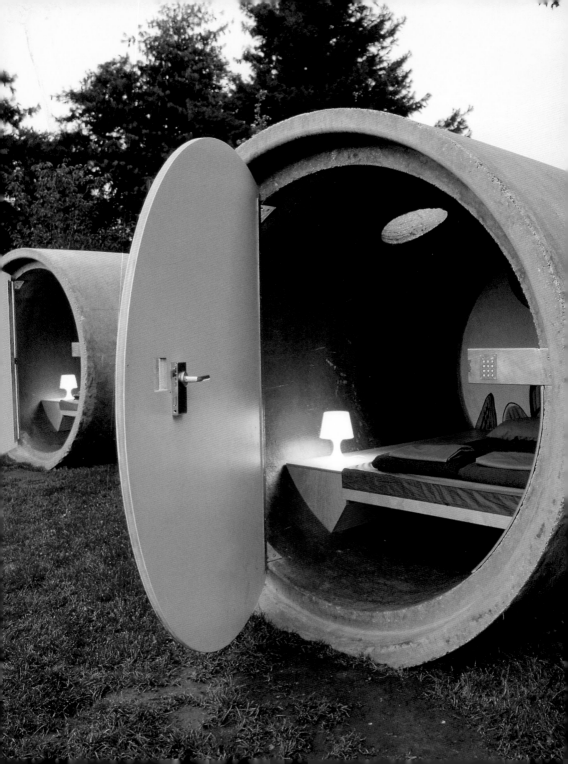

DAS PARK HOTEL
Sleep in a concrete pipe

DAS PARK HOTEL ❿
Ottensheim
Near Linz
Austria
online information only
www.dasparkhotel.net

ROOMS AND RATES
Three double-room pipes.
There are currently three
tubes, with an honesty
box for contributions
towards the upkeep. €20
would be an acceptable
minimum for a night, but
leaving €40 ensures that
this art project can benefit
the community and be
developed at other locations.

LOCATION
Ottensheim is a short taxi
ride from nearby Linz,
and the tubes are located
in the Donauradweg park,
next to the Danube.

Although Das Park is a one-off hotel, it has been designed from the outset to use worldwide standard concrete drainage or sewage pipe sections – so you could well see more of them in the future.

The idea of Andreas Strauss, the first rooms were built after the idea received sponsorship from the concrete tube manufacturer. The beauty of these pipes is that the utilitarian look needs little alteration to make them habitable – a coat of varnish is all that's necessary. The tubes have also had wall paintings by the Austrian artist Thomas Latzel Ochoa to make them seem a little more user-friendly. After a season or two, they can even be returned to the manufacturer for reuse, as the bed, door and lock mechanism, as well as the lighting and internet access, are all easy to remove. Like cave hotels, Das Park Hotel is cool in the summer, and perhaps still warm in winter, although at the moment the hotel is only open from May to October.

Each tube weighs 9 ½ tons – so although some people might be tempted to rock or vandalize them, they are incredibly robust and need little maintenance. You do however need a hefty crane to lift them into place.

Rooms are accessed by a digital lock, whose code is provided by the self-service website upon booking acceptance. Once inside, facilities are functional but basic – a double bed, light, power point, blanket and the light cotton sleeping bag provided are all you need for a night in a concrete tube.

The toilet and showers are a couple of minutes' walk away, details on booking.

ALMDORF SEINERZEIT TREEHOUSE

A love nest facing the valley

ALMDORF SEINERZEIT ⑪
Fellacheralm
A-9564 Patergassen
Carinthie, Austria
+434275-7201
office@almdorf.com

ROOMS AND RATES
From €490 per night
for the wedding lodge

Located 30 minutes from Villach, Almdorf Seinerzeit is a small paradise of a dozen or so chalets, each of which has two or three bedrooms. Here, you can rent an entire lodge or chalet, not just one room. All are elegantly designed and decorated (nothing flashy, just authentic wood and stone), but one chalet stands out: it has an additional little cabin set up in a tree facing the valley.

The cabin, connected by a drawbridge which, once drawn up, leaves you completely cut off from the world, is equipped with all modern comforts despite its small size. You'll just have to decide at which temperature to set the heating so you're not too hot or too cold to fully admire the beautiful view of the valley through the large bay window. Candles and matches are left at your disposal to create the perfect romantic setting. In addition to a traditional restaurant, Almdorf also has an astonishing and delightful hut that claims to be "the smallest restaurant in the world". This charming site allows a maximum of four people to dine facing the valley in an atmosphere that is quite enchanting thanks to the wood fire that the chef uses from time to time to prepare the meal (the rest of the time, you'll be alone in the tranquil hut).

To better appreciate the experience, before dinner we suggest trying the mountain herbal bath at the hotel spa (if you can stand water at more than 40 °C / 105 °F). In an extremely warm atmosphere (the decoction of herbs is brought to a near boil in a copper cauldron set over a wood fire in a huge stone fireplace), you rest on a bed of straw to relax as you regain your spirits.

JAIL HOTEL

First prison conversion in Switzerland

JAILHOTEL LÖWENGRABEN **⑫**
Löwengraben 18
CH - 6004 Luzern,
Switzerland
+41 41 410 7830
hotel@jailhotel.ch
www.jailhotel.ch

ROOMS AND RATES
56 rooms and suites.
Rooms (except Unplugged),
are equipped with private
shower, toilet and sink. Basic
Unplugged rooms are from
CHF90 (Swiss francs) for a
single room, with a simple
twin CHF130. The popular
Most Wanted rooms are
CHF130 for a double or twin
room. Theme suites are from
CHF190–220 per room. All
rooms are non-smoking
and prices include buffet
breakfast and city taxes.

LOCATION
Close to the railway station,
there is a public parking
garage called "Altstadt"
(www.parking-luzern.
ch) only 5 minutes walk
from the hotel for guests
arriving by car. Special cards
for public parking spaces
in the city of Lucerne are
available at reception.

The Jail hotel is located in the heart of Lucerne, right in the centre of the Old Town only a few minutes from the lake. This former prison was built in 1862 and was converted into a prison hotel in 1999, the first in Switzerland. It's a great budget choice for visitors and offers a number of conference rooms and business facilities. A total of fifty-six different rooms and suites are offered from original "Unplugged" rooms where you have a bunk bed and more authentic prison experience, to the larger "Most Wanted" rooms, and largest Theme suites of Prison Governor, Library, Barabas and Falling Water. The thick walls, solid doors and barred windows retain their original feel, although none of the rooms are huge and private bathrooms are small, with shower. The Unplugged rooms have their private shower across the corridor.

There aren't any lifts, so if you're concerned about stairs or

have heavy bags, ask for one of the rooms on the lower floors. Also be aware that on Saturday the nightclub adjoining the hotel hosts a party night, so expect a little more noise than usual. The nightclub is open from Thursday to Saturday, 11pm until 5am. Entry to the disco is free for hotel residents.

LA CLAUSTRA

Sleep luxuriously in a former secret military underground installation

LA CLAUSTRA ⓑ
San Gottardo
CH-6780 Airolo, Switzerland
+41 91 880 5055
info@claustra.ch
www.claustra.ch

ROOMS AND RATES
17 double rooms.
Daily rates per person for
the seventeen bedrooms are
from around CHF245 (Swiss
francs) (US$210 / €170)

LOCATION
La Claustra is halfway
between Zurich and Milan
and can be reached by car or
public transport from either
city in around 2 hours.
Open between May
and October.

When the Swiss army gave up their Alpine fortifications in 1999, artist Jean Odermatt saw the opportunity and created the Fondazione La Claustra. Opened in 2004, La Claustra is hewn deep into the rock and provides both a hotel and creative laboratory situated among some of the most stunning scenery, with views of the rooftop of Europe. Each of the seventeen rooms is embedded inside the mountain and provides simple tranquil settings for quiet reflection. En suite bathroom facilities are fed directly by the five sources of water harnessed within the St Gotthard region, which provide 7% of Europe's drinking water. La Claustra also provides a Wellness Oasis, spa-fed direct from the springs, with a steam bath in a unique glass cube, bordered by *kusatsu* pools for relaxation. A number of meeting rooms and common spaces have been provided in the caverns of this underground property, including hi-tech conference rooms which are in demand during the summer months for company events and workshops.

Achtung
Türen sofort schliessen
Hebel sichern.
Attenzione
Chiudere subito le porte
E assicurare le leve

WHITEPOD

Hi-tech igloos in a Swiss eco resort

WHITEPOD ⓮
Les Cerniers
Batt. Postale 681
1871 Les Giettes - Switzerland
+41 24 471 38 38
reservations@whitepod.com
www.whitepod.com
Fifteen pods available

ROOMS AND RATES
From CHF400
Midweek, to CHF590 at
weekends, based on single
or double occupancy
and subject to
a two-night minimum stay

LOCATION
The resort is above
"Les Cerniers", a small village
at the foot of the Dents du
Midi. The nearest town is
Aigle, where you should
aim if you're travelling
by train from Geneva,
or if arriving by TGV.

Whitepod is the creation of Swiss-born Sofia de Meyer, who wanted a high-tech solution to the challenge of creating a different, eco-friendly way of catching up with yourself in the natural beauty of the Swiss Alps.

Now in its third year, the resort has left little mark on the environment, but made a great mark in ecotourism – winning the Responsible Tourism Award for Innovation.

The fifteen geodesic dome pods that make up Whitepod have been equipped with traditional furnishings and a simple wood-burning stove that keeps you comfortably warm. The pods are lit by lanterns and the only electricity is in the main chalet 3 or 4 minutes' walk away. Covered with white canvas in the winter and green in the summer, they blend perfectly into the surrounding landscape. The pods themselves are built on wooden platforms, so they can be moved easily. The main chalet houses the dining and spa facilities as well as the bathrooms, although the larger pavilion pods have en suite facilities.

The view of the mountains opposite, from the large bedroom window of the pod, is stunning, even more so when the sunlight reflects off the snow to wake you up in the morning. No need for an alarm clock here. After time on the private ski run with three lifts and 7 km (4 miles) of piste, or a traditional snow-shoe randonnée (ramble) in the nearby forests, you sleep soundly and wake early – but refreshed. Perhaps it is the clear mountain air or the fondue of the previous night, but you seem to have energy that was lacking when you arrived. This outdoor effort also builds up an appetite and the resident chef provides two nightly menus, one with traditionally hearty Swiss mountain food such as raclette and fondue, the other with lighter dishes using locally sourced ingredients. Such is the integration with the community, that Whitepod even runs a small grocery store for villagers.

IGLU-DORF

Sleep in an artist igloo or build your own!

Iglu-Dorf GmbH ⑮
Rotzbergstrasse 15
6362 Stansstad - Switzerland
+41 41 612 27 28
info@iglu-dorf.com
www.iglu-dorf.com

ROOMS AND RATES
Forty-two to sixty-two rooms, depending on the village. Available in locations in the Swiss Alps and in Zugspitze, villages accommodate up to thirty-eight guests in different igloo options from standard and "Romantic" igloos for two, to larger family and group igloos. Prices are lowest midweek, rising at weekends and during the New Year. They include food, non-alcoholic beverages and the use of sauna or whirlpool facilities. One night midweek in the standard igloo is from CHF149. The most inexpensive romantic igloo can be booked for CHF249 (€166) per person, while weekend nights in the top-range "Romantic plus" suites cost around CHF529 (€349) per person, per night at the weekend.

Adrian Günter built his first igloo in 1996, to better enjoy the mountain and first powder snow of the day. Following an avalanche of interest from friends wanting to sample an igloo night, he increased the number of igloos and opened the "small world in white" in 2004, with five villages across Switzerland and Germany now accepting guests.

Moving 3,000 tons of snow every December to build each village, Adrian invites Inuit artists from Canada to craft sculptures inside each village. With only an ice pick, motor saw and shovel, artists produce seals, arctic wolves, polar bears and whales as well as swirling designs and patterns illuminated by candlelight to overlook the guests from the walls.

The villages are open from Christmas Day to the beginning of April each year, snow conditions permitting. With 5,600 visitors in 2006, all ages have enjoyed the cosy hospitality of an expedition sleeping bag and sheepskin rug, from the youngest 19-month-old baby to an 83-year-old lady guest.

A variety of igloo options are available in the different villages, from standard and group igloos to "Romantic" suites with private whirlpool or sauna. The team have even built a church, including an altar and baptismal font for a wedding party. Every village is equipped with a large igloo hotel lobby and bar where the evening meal of Gruyère fondue and mulled wine is served. The top-range "Romantic-plus" igloos include their own toilet, although you'll not want to spend too long sitting on the seat!

HÔTEL PALAFITTE

Hotel on stilts, in the heart of Switzerland

HÔTEL PALAFITTE 16
Route des Gouttes d'Or 2
Neuchâtel
CH-2000
Switzerland
+41 32 723 02 02
reservation@palafitte.ch
www.palafitte.ch

ROOMS AND RATES
Twenty-four suites built
directly over the lake.
Lakeside pavilions from
CHF505 (US$415 / €300) to
CHF680 (US$560 / €410).
The shore-based pavilions
are cheaper at CHF385-490
(US$320-410 / €235-300)
but don't share the lake
access from the terrace.

LOCATION
The hotel is on the outskirts
of the town, about
10 minutes to the main
shopping area by public bus.
The hotel provides a free
shuttle bus for guests to and
from the railway station.

Although the Swiss are known worldwide for their fine chocolate and engineering excellence, unusual hotels do not immediately spring to mind. Hôtel Palafitte connects the quality tastes of the discerning Swiss with something a little bit different – rooms built directly over Neuchâtel Lake, with private terraces and ladders dipping into the water for guests.

All the lakeside apartments are staggered so that they have an unobstructed view of the lake – from just about everywhere in the room – even the bath! Your privacy is assured as none of the rooms have direct views of the other rooms. The rooms themselves are impressively furnished with the latest gadgets, hi-tech TV, computer and sound systems. Don't forget to ask how everything works when you're shown your room otherwise you'll spend your evening reading manuals or calling reception for instructions.

The night view of the moon shimmering on the lake with the Alps in the distance is very impressive and the morning sunrise is stunning. While the rooms on the shore are perfectly adequate, it's worth the additional cost of the lakeside room to enjoy the view and private terrace.

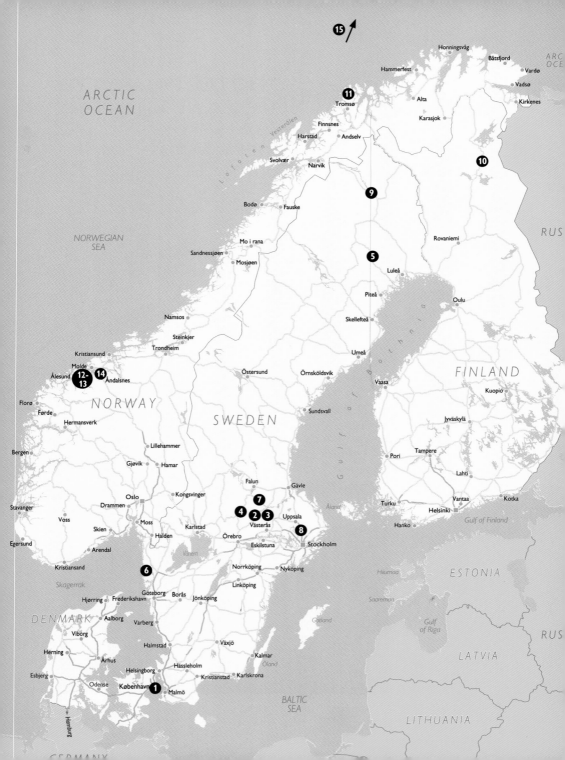

SCANDINAVIA

ROOM 606 AT THE RADISSON BLU ROYAL HOTEL

The only Arne Jacobsen room left

ROOM 606 AT THE RADISSON BLU ROYAL HOTEL ❶
Hammerichsgade 1
DK-1611 Copenhagen,
Denmark
+45 33 426000
www.radissonblu.com/
royalhotel-copenhagen/
rooms/room-606

ROOMS AND RATES
DKK4,900 (Danish kroner)
per night, breakfast
included (about €650)

Built in the 1960s following the launch of transatlantic airlines, the Radisson Blu Royal Hotel was entirely designed by Danish design icon Arne Jacobsen.

At the time of its creation this was Copenhagen's first skyscraper and Scandinavia's largest hotel, and it has since been renovated several times. In the 80s, all the furniture was changed, but the hotel had the happy idea of preserving some of it in order to recreate, among other features, one of the designer rooms, with the original furniture, textiles, chandeliers, lamps and cutlery.

Unlike the rest of the hotel furnishings, which includes recent copies, room 606 is the last remaining demonstration of Arne Jacobsen's entire design, as everything is authentic.

If, like us, you generally don't appreciate chain hotels, make an exception: beyond its historic nature and vintage feel, the room also offers a lovely view of the city. You'll feel just fine here.

HOTEL UTTER INN

Sleep inside a floating aquarium, where the fish look in and you look out

Hotel Utter Inn ❷
Underwater hotel
Kopparbergsvägen 1,
721 87 Västerås
Sweden
+46 21 39 01 00
malarstaden@vasteras.se
www.vasterasmalarstaden.se

ROOMS AND RATES
One cosy bedroom for two
1,500 kronor per person
per night, including dinner
and breakfast (US$220 /
€165). The hotel opens at
the beginning of April and
the season runs through
to late September.

LOCATION
Your prearranged boat ride
leaves from Västerås tourist
port, about 40 minutes by
train from central Stockholm,
or 10 minutes by car from
the low-cost airline gateway
airport of Västerås.

For the ultimate seclusion for the night, consider sleeping in this underwater hotel in the middle of Lake Mälaren, 1 km (1/2 mile) from Västerås. Your room is reached by a water-taxi ride to a small hut on a floating steel platform moored a short distance from one of the outlying islands. There is a terrace with a couple of chairs. Inside, the giant steel hatch dominates the room and the rest of the space is taken up by a toilet (thankfully), cooker, small heater and some storage space. After a few brief instructions you're left to the solitude that artist Mikael Genberg originally intended the Utter (Otter) Inn to emphasize. Climb down the steps and your twin bedroom awaits, 3 m (10 ft) below the surface of the lake. Not a place for those scared of enclosed spaces, as once the hatch shuts you are very much in a different world, floating in an aquarium with four picture windows for the aquatic inhabitants to look in at you – and you to peek out.

Furnishings are simple (from IKEA of course). Two beds, a small table and a couple of low-voltage reading lights or a candle lantern for illumination.

A picnic dinner and breakfast are included in the deluxe

package and after relaxing on the terrace chairs you retire below. It's eerily silent and as darkness finally falls you are gently rocked to sleep. The only noisy neighbours are the ones you choose to arrive with. Woken by the wake of an early-morning ferry shaking the hotel, you see a large pike that's been observing you as if window-shopping for a snack later on.

Pick your companion wisely as there is no escape from snoring in a steel box underwater!

HOTEL HACKSPETT

A self-contained treehouse in a city-centre location

HÔTEL HACKSPETT ❸
Kopparbergsvägen 1
721 87 Västerås,
Sweden
+46 21 39 01 00
malarstaden@vasteras.se
www.vasterasmalarstaden.se

ROOMS AND RATES
One cosy bedroom for two
1,500 kronor per person
per night, including dinner
and breakfast (US$220 /
€165). The hotel opens at
the beginning of April and
the season runs through
to late September.

LOCATION
The treehouse is in the
centre of Västerås city park,
and most guests meet at
the Västerås tourist office,
about 40 minutes by train
from central Stockholm, or
10 minutes by car from the
low-cost airline gateway
airport of Västerås.

Thirteen metres (42 ft) is a long way up any tree, let alone a 130-year-old oak in the central park of Västerås near Stockholm. The Hotel Hackspett (Woodpecker) is another extraordinary brainchild of Mikael Genberg, artist and innovator of this hotel and its sister, the underwater Utter (Otter) Inn on nearby Lake Mälaren.

Reached via a sturdy but wobbly rope ladder, the platform has an impressive view of the park below and out to the lake beyond. Advice to "pack light" was appreciated as your luggage is hoisted up on a rope from the tree-house platform.

On arrival you discover your picnic supper and breakfast packs waiting. There is the briefest of tours covering safety and operation of the most essential item at the top of a tree – a toilet. Pull up the rope ladder and you retire to find the treehouse well thought out and equipped. From an IKEA bed and duvet, heater and cooking facilities, Mikael has anticipated your needs. There are even a few books on a shelf and a small lantern to read by.

Surprisingly you never quite escape the background noise of the city centre, but the rustle of leaves and sound of children playing football below is rather calming. Your mind is at peace when you're sitting quietly in a tree, although not enough to appreciate birdsong from the crack of dawn. It's surprising how loud birds are when you're at their level!

At night, the only reminder of civilization is the faint roar of traffic on the road far below. If you really want peace and solitude however, don't forget to turn off your mobile phone – coverage is rather good from this treetop vantage point.

KOLARBYN

Sleep in a "camouflage" hut in the woods, with no electricity

KOLARBYN ❹
Skinnskatteberg
Bergslagen
Sweden
+46 70 40 070 53
andreas@kolarbyn.se
www.kolarbyn.se

ROOMS AND RATES
Kolarbyn eco-lodge is open
for individual guests from 1
May to 30 September. Rates
for adults are 350 kronor
per person (US$38 / €27),
with children half price.
Prices for lodging include
a sleeping mat, sheepskin
rug, wood to cut for your
fire, candles, matches, fresh
water (to fetch yourself
from the well) and access
to fireplaces for cooking.
Kolarbyn recommend that
you bring you own sleeping
bag. You should also bring
a torch and pillow.

LOCATION
Kolarbyn is a couple of hours
by car from Stockholm and
45 minutes from Västerås.
Trains run hourly from
Stockholm Central Station
to Köping, where there is
a public bus connection
to Skinnskatteberg for an
arranged pick-up by the
Kolarbyn team. Travel
time is about 2 hours 20
minutes. Tickets may be
purchased at train stations;
on-line booking of train
and bus tickets is cheaper.

Kolarbyn consists of twelve little forest huts located by the beautiful Lake Skärsjön. Known as Sweden's most primitive hotel, the huts have no electricity and the dark evenings are lit by candles or traditional oil lamps. Each hut provides two berths with sheepskin rugs to cushion your slumber. You're kept warm by a wood heater, and your first task is to gather and chop enough wood for your cooking and heating needs.

During the week guests bring food to cook themselves at one of several fireplaces — one even has a view over the lake. The nearest supermarket is 3 km away at Skinnskatteberg, and pans and cutlery are available in the storehouse. At weekends, food can be provided for those making a reservation in advance.

There is also a sauna to chop wood for, although as washing facilities are limited to a stream, you are encouraged to be brave enough to cool down with a dip in the nearby lake.

Toilets are in natural outhouses which, though rustic, serve their purpose adequately, as was the normal practice for centuries!

TREEHOTEL
Treehouses in a woodland setting

TreeHotel ❺
Edeforsvägen 2A
960 24 Harads, Sweden
+46 928 104 03
info@treehotel.se
www.treehotel.se

Rooms and rates
6 separate treehouses from
SEK3500 (€390) to SEK4200
(€470) on a double use basis.

Location
Treehotel is located in
the beautiful village of
Harads, in the Norrbotten
region of northern Sweden,
approximately 80 km
(50 miles, 1 hour by car)
from Luleå airport (the
largest airport in northern
Sweden), 47 km (29 miles)
upstream from Boden. It
is approximately 60 km
(37 miles) south of the Arctic
Circle. With a population
of around 600, Harads has
restaurants, stores, hostel,
fuel station, swimming
facilities, viewing areas, as
well as a beautiful church.

This stunning treetop accommodation in Harads in northern Sweden was designed with the help of six well-known designers and architects, who turned their ideas into unique treehouses, created in harmony with nature and their ecological values.

All the treehouses are sited in pine trees between 4–6 m (13–20 ft) from the ground. The rooms can be accessed either by a ramp or sturdy steps. One of them has an electric, retractable stepladder.

They each have their own living and sleeping areas with between two and four beds. In addition there is a sauna and a relaxing room seating twelve guests comfortably. This is the first tree hotel with a sauna!

SALT & SILL

Floating hotel and sauna

SALT & SILL ❻
Salt & Co AB
471 51 Klädesholmen
Tjörn, Sweden
+46 304 67 34 80
info@saltosill.se
www.saltosill.se

ROOMS AND RATES
23 rooms including one suite.
From SEK1990 to SEK2190 for
a double room and SEK2690
to SEK3290 for the suite.
The suite is located at the top
far end of the hotel and offers
a fantastic view over the fjord
and the island of Flatholmen.
Suite guests have the benefit
of a roof-top jacuzzi.

LOCATION
Only 45 minutes by car
from Gothenburg, you're
guaranteed sea views over
Bohuslän's outer archipelago.

At the western tip of Tjörn, on Klädesholmen island, you'll find Salt & Sill, Sweden's first floating hotel. It's the idea of owners Susanna and Patrick Hermansson who, in 2004, dreamed of starting a business offering a complete experience with food, drink and accommodation, built around the peaceful island of Klädesholmen. Unfortunately, the limited space on the island meant there was only one way to make it happen – they had to build a floating hotel, consisting of six two-storey buildings on pontoons.

Now permanently moored next to the acclaimed *Salt & Sill* restaurant, facilities include bedrooms, a suite, terrace area and conference facilities, as well as a separate floating sauna. The sauna is a miniature copy of the main hotel, powered by two 160 hp Volvo Penta diesel engines, reaching speeds of up to 15 knots. It can be used as a relaxation area, conference room, and wedding suite.

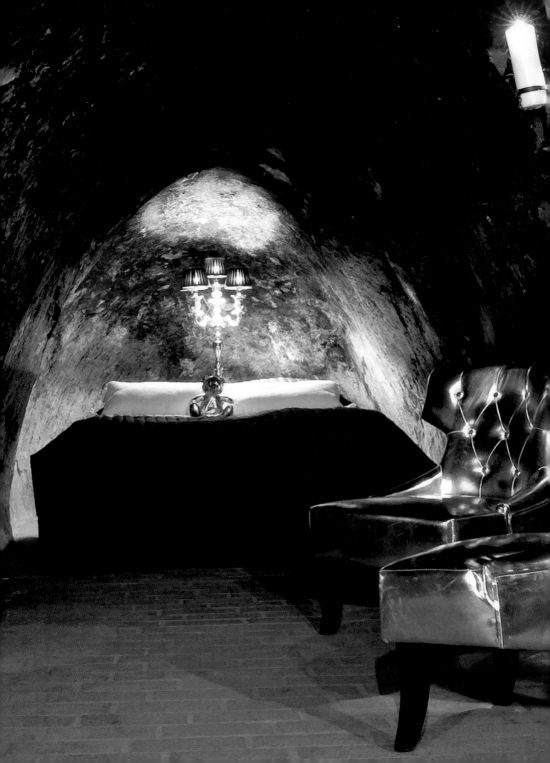

SALA SILVERMINE UNDERGROUND SUITE

The world's deepest bedroom suite in an undergound silver mine

SALA SILVERGRUVA ❼
Sala
Västmanland, Sweden
+46 224 677 260
booking@salasilvergruva.se
www.salasilvergruva.se

ROOMS AND RATES
One suite.
The single underground
suite costs SEK3,990
(Swedish kronor) for two
people (including taxes).
Included in this price is a
guided tour of the –155 m
level, your refreshments
basket, breakfast and stay
in the mining suite.
Wear warm and comfortable
clothes for the underground
tours. Year-round, it is
only 2 degrees Celsius. The
underground festivity hall
and suite are warmed up to
18 degrees and the bed is
equipped with a thick cover
and an extra pair of blankets.
The mine staff are available
above ground throughout
the night and you're given
an intercom radio through
which you can communicate.
Mobile phones do not work at
155 m underground, so if you
need to be contacted, please
ask them to ring the mine's
general phone number.

LOCATION
Sala Silvermine is situated
in central Sweden in the
Västmanland region,
120 km (75 miles) from
Stockholm, 62 km (39
miles) from Uppsala, 37 km
(23 miles) from Västerås,
81 km (50 miles) from
Eskilstuna and 114 km
(71 miles) from Falun.

Sleep 155 m (510 ft) underground in the historic Sala Silvermine, one of the world's best-preserved mine settings. Here you'll see dark winding galleries and vast lake-filled caverns. Even to those not familiar with mining, the underground setting is sensational, especially when you consider it was entirely created by human hands. It is cold, damp and dark, but very beautiful, if not a little scary.

After a guided tour of the –155 m underground level, you are provided with a basket of refreshments and something to drink. The Sala mine guide then leaves you alone in your suite below ground to enjoy the refreshments and the quiet of the mine. In the morning a guide comes to serve your breakfast before you're taken to ground level again.

Showers are in the above-ground hostel, which was originally built as a rooming house for unmarried men around 1920 and is decorated in 1920s and 1950s styles. It is also available for overnight accommodation.

JUMBO STAY

Sleep in the cockpit of a 747

JUMBO STAY ❽
Arlanda Airport
Stockholm, Sweden
+46 8 593 604 00
booking@jumbohostel.com
www.jumbostay.com/

ROOMS AND RATES
The Cockpit Suite is SEK3,300 (Swedish kronor) for couples, breakfast included. It features two adjustable beds, a flatscreen TV, free wireless internet and a private bathroom with shower. If the cockpit is taken, try out the BlackBox room at the back of the plane. It's a great option for visitors to Stockholm staying several nights as it's cheaper at SEK1,900 (SEK950 per person), breakfast included.
The dormitory-style bedrooms are equipped with a variety of 90 cm (3 ft) beds or one 90 cm and one 140 cm (4.5 ft) bed according to occupancy. Prices per person are from SEK350 for the four-beds to SEK450 for the two-beds. Breakfast is an additional SEK65.

LOCATION
You can hardly stay closer to the airport as the plane is only a short walk from the check-in counters at Arlanda. It's ideal for anyone catching an early flight who doesn't want to get out of bed before dawn to make it to the airport in time – or families with children who want an extraordinary beginning to their holidays.

This 1976 vintage jumbo jet guarantees a memorable night for guests in a variety of room options, from shared low-cost dormitories to a couple of luxury suites, one in the cockpit and the other in the tail.

The dormitory rooms have single, twin, three-bed and four-bed combinations with shared shower and toilet in the corridor. They're comfortable and clean and perfect for those with early flights at the airport.

The luxury suites are much more of a treat and the converted cockpit provides a view of the airport taxiway.

You're guaranteed a unique and outstanding experience for all budgets.

ICE HOTEL

Sleep at −5 °C in an ephemeral work of art

ICE HOTEL ❾
981 91 Jukkasjärvi, Sweden
+46 980 668 00
E-mail: info@icehotel.com
www.icehotel.com

ROOMS AND RATES
Around eighty rooms
(number varies
from year to year)
From €200 for a
standard room and
from €300 for a suite

LOCATION
A 30-minute drive from
the town of Kiruna. If the
Stockholm-Kiruna flight
is fully booked or too
expensive, you can take the
direct-link night train.

Although the Icehotel has become a classic of the unexpected and has featured in most of the world's magazines (Kate Moss and Naomi Campbell have been photographed here), it's still an undefinable place that will satisfy the most curious among you – and the least sensitive to the cold!

The peculiar feature of this hotel, first created in the early 1990s, is that it is (re)built every year at the beginning of winter with the frozen water of the nearby river, and it melts every spring. The cycle is complete: the river water turns to ice and then returns naturally to the river some six months later...

The Icehotel offers two types of accommodation: bedrooms or suites. In both cases you sleep on a block of ice covered with an insulating sheet and reindeer skins and the ambient temperature is around −5 °C. As the suites are all designed by different artists, if you have the means don't hesitate to book one of them; the impression of sleeping in an actual work of art is quite extraordinary.

The hotel also offers the famous and indispensable Icebar, open to non-residents, as well as an ice chapel sought out by some couples as a likely venue to get married. Although all this seems idyllic on paper, the sleeping bags are not always up to the task: if you want to avoid being wakened around 6 in the morning feeling cold, bring your own severe-weather sleeping bag. Also bring your warmest clothes, even if you'll probably wear the jumpsuit that the hotel kindly hands out to guests on arrival.

Finally, beware of the "warm rooms": they're comfortable but quite expensive and have no bathtub.

Of the two restaurants near the hotel, we strongly recommend the one furthest away: it is in a much more charming setting and the walk is very pleasant (see following page on aurora borealis).

SEE THE AURORA BOREALIS

The aurora borealis phenomenon occurs frequently but isn't visible every day. So don't be disappointed if you happen to be there at a bad time.

If the sky is clear, you'll need to go some distance from the hotel lights. A great idea is to walk to the second restaurant in the village, via the frozen lake. The walk (around 15 minutes) is magnificent at night when the conditions are optimal for seeing the northern lights.

HITCHHIKE TO KIRUNA IN –35 °C

Despite what you might think, hitchhiking can be a good way of getting to Kiruna: cars pass fairly frequently and the cold, though intense (the outside temperature averages –35 °C), is perfectly bearable for a few minutes if you're well wrapped up, as the air is very dry. Another plus is that you won't have to wait 20 minutes for a taxi at the hotel. Because of the climate, passing drivers rarely fail to stop...

THINGS TO DO

Whatever happens don't miss going out on a dog-sledging expedition. Allow at least two days to taste the magic of the polar nights.

Mats Peterson is especially recommended: you'll drive your own sled pulled by four dogs and sleep at his place, in an insulated wooden cabin in the middle of nowhere.

Mats is an experienced sledger: he was even chosen to organize an outing for the king and queen of Sweden.

At Kiruna, visits to the iron-ore mine and the wooden church, a Swedish national monument.

HOTEL KAKSLAUTTANEN

Unique glass igloos to see the Aurora Borealis in comfort

HOTEL KAKSLAUTTENEN ⑩
FI-99830 Saariselkä
Lapland - Finland
+358 16 667 100
hotel@kakslauttanen.fi
www.kakslauttanen.fi

ROOMS AND RATES

Thirty two log cabins, twenty snow igloos and twenty glass igloos. Snow igloos on a half-board basis are from €200 per person per night, or around €312 for a couple sharing. Glass igloos on a couple-sharing basis are around €368 half board for two. There are discounts for children and longer stays and special programme prices apply for Christmas and the New Year.

LOCATION

The closest airport is Ivalo Airport, about 40 km (25 miles) away. The hotel can arrange car or snowmobile transfers. For reference, Helsinki is 1,085 km (674 miles) away and the nearest ATM is in Saariselka village, 10 km (6 miles) away.

In order to marvel at the amazing Northern Lights, Hotel Kakslauttanen provides a choice of futuristic glass igloos as well as traditional snow igloo and wood cabin accommodation. While snow igloos are a winter speciality, the glass igloos are available all year round. The first five glass igloos were opened in 2004 and such was guest feedback that a further fifteen were built in 2006.

Using temperature-resistant glass, these igloos keep the inside warm, while the outside is −30 °C. This allows you to lie in bed and, if you're lucky, see the amazing Aurora Borealis lightshow. This natural phenomenon usually appears in the night sky between the end of August and April, however peak activity is around April and September.

For more traditional winter fun, Hotel Kakslauttanen offers log cabins all year round and snow igloos from late December to April. As with all snow and ice hotel accommodation, the interior is cool, typically between −3 °C and −6 °C, and you'll need the warm sleeping bag provided so you don't feel the cold.

VULKANA

Fishing boat conversion

VULKANA DRIFT SØNDRE ⑪
Tollbodgate 3A9008
Tromsø, Norway
+47 911 00 626
post@vulkana.no
www.vulkana.no

ROOMS AND RATES
Up to twelve guests can
be accommodated.
There are three cabins
with double beds in the
aft of the vessel. In the
bow there is a traditional
cabin with four beds.
A single cabin costs from
NOK995 (Norwegian
kroner), double NOK1,490,
triple NOK1,790, and a
four-person room NOK1,990,
inclusive of taxes.
Hot tub, sauna and steam
room / hamam are
additionally charged, for
the whole group to use.
Packages that include
sea-faring trips to secluded
bays are also available.

Vulkana isn't a traditional hotel. Originally a 23 m (75 ft) whaler built in 1957, it was transformed by a group of enthusiasts and architect Sami Rintala in 2008 into a base for relaxation.

While still retaining ocean-going abilities and refurbished cabins, the ship now includes a sauna, hamam steam room and on-deck hot tub.

Sitting in a saltwater hot tub while travelling through the wild Arctic nature is an amazing experience, no matter whether the midnight sun or the northern lights fill the sky.

SVINØY FYR

Remote island retreat

SVINØY FYR ⑫
62NORD AS
Skansekaia
N-6002 Ålesund, Norway
+47 7011 4433
post@62.no
www.62.no

ROOMS AND RATES
Accommodates up to
eleven in four double
and three single rooms

LOCATION
The lighthouse is located
12 nautical miles off the
Norwegian coast in the
open ocean in an area
renowned locally for some
of the wildest weather
that Norway can offer.
The island is reachable by
boat, but due to the power
and unpredictability of the
waves, for safety reasons
the management provides
access by helicopter only.

Svinøy is a unique environment in one of the most distinctive and unusual locations in the world. Its rugged beauty and solitude are for those who want to experience something really exclusive.

The (now automated) lighthouse was manned for 100 years, from 1905 to 2005, and has been a meteorological observation since 1955. Weather data from Svinøy lighthouse are still vital for the overall meteorological data image. Svinøy can accommodate up to eleven visitors (four double rooms plus three single rooms).

You have the entire 900 m (3,000 ft) long island to yourself, staying in the house which once was utilized by the lighthouse keepers.

Pricing is entirely based upon your requirements, and includes helicopter transport and a permanent staff member/cook who will accompany you.

MOLJA FYR

Tiny, harbour entrance lighthouse in Ålesund

HOTEL BROSUNDET ⑬
Apotekergata 56004
Ålesund, Norway
+ 47 7011 4500
post@brosundet.no
www.brosundet.no

ROOMS AND RATES
One double room for
Nok 4.500, (€600) - per
night, including fruit and
champagne upon arrival, and
breakfast served at the door.

The interior of the 150-year-old lighthouse is completely round and only 3 m (10 ft) in diameter, but through effective use of the available space, Molja now boasts a bedroom upstairs and a bathroom downstairs.

The interior design was carried out by Snohetta, Norway's best-known architects (designers of the Oslo Opera House and Ground Zero museum in New York City among many other landmark projects). They have carefully achieved a wonderfully distinctive blend of modern facilities within a historic building while keeping the rustic character of the property.

Molja Fyr is managed by the nearby forty-six-room Hotel Brosundet, located in a 100-year-old protected building. As a result, Molja Fyr has become known locally as "Room 47" of the boutique property. Full hotel facilities are available at the main hotel, including the Maki Restaurant, which has established a superb reputation for its fresh seafood.

The lighthouse itself is positioned at the end of a 100 m (330 ft) sea wall, creating an experience that is entirely unique, as you are able to experience the seclusion of a tiny building facing the power of nature, while at the same time staying very close to the centre of town.

Some guests say that it's even more of an experience to visit during a winter storm than to stay on a beautiful summer's day.

JUVET™ LANDSKAPSHOTELL

A minimalist room looking out to the colourful ancient forest

Juvet™ landskapshotell 🏴
Alstad
6210 Valldal, Norway
+47 950 32 010
post@juvet.com
www.juvet.com

Rooms and rates
Double room with breakfast:
NOK1,250 per person per day

Location
A 2 hour transfer from
Ålesund Vigra airport to
the hotel can be arranged,
or fly to Oslo Gardermoen
Airport and then take the
train to Åndalsnes. There
is a bus from Åndalsnes
across the Trollstigen to
Gudbrandsjuvet, where
the hotel can arrange
to pick you up.

Turning design hotel convention on its head, Juvet – Europe's first "landscape hotel" – offers guests an understated, dark and bare room interior to enhance the natural landscape views from the panoramic windows.

As the head architect of Oslo-based designers Jensen & Skodvin explains, "We wanted to give the feeling that you're outside even though you're protected inside."

At first, these minimalist pine and glass-clad buildings may seem haphazardly constructed, yet the views from their panoramic windows highlight that their locations have been expertly and specifically oriented to a particular vista. Some overlook the surrounding birch, aspen and pine forest, while others focus on nature-sculpted boulders, providing serenity as in a traditional Zen garden. You can almost feel the trees brushing against you, and the snow-white drops of spray from the River Valldøla on your face.

BASECAMP EXPLORER

Sleep like Shackleton, locked in ice

BASECAMP EXPLORER 🄯
Basecamp Spitsbergen
P.O. Box 316
9171 Longyearbyen, Norway
+47 79 02 46 00
svalbard@
basecampexplorer.com
www.basecampexplorer.com

ROOMS AND RATES
Ten cabins with twenty beds.
An overnight package
to include food and
snowmobile transit from
Longyerbyn is NOK 7.990,
(€1100)- per driver/
NOK 6.190, (€820)- per
passenger on a shared basis

LOCATION
Starting from Longyearbyen
you'll reach the *Noorderlicht*
by dog sled or snow scooter
transit. This is a 7 km
(4.5 mile) journey. You're
advised to wrap up really well
as temperatures vary between
−10 and −30 degrees Celsius.
You'll be accompanied by an
experienced armed guard as
while the romantic notion
of polar bears is a pleasant
fairy story, the reality is that
these magnificent creatures
are dangerous in the wild
if disturbed … or hungry.

Launched in 1910 and originally built as a lightship in the Baltic, since 2004 this steel sailing schooner *Noorderlicht* has been frozen every year in the winter fjord ice of Tempelfjord, Spitzbergen. This fjord is one of the easternmost fjords inside Isfjorden and is surrounded by temple-shaped mountains from which it takes its name.

Life aboard the only hotel boat frozen in sea ice is a unique experience as you get to experience Arctic nature right up close and personal.

The sounds of nature, from the movement of ice and the rush of wind to the complete silence of a blue sky-filled day can be both relaxing and unnerving. The light is equally extreme – from 24-hour darkness where with luck you'll see the northern lights, to the first glimmer of sun in spring, with beautiful pink and orange skies.

The ship also offers a fantastic view of "Von Post" Glacier.

ACKNOWLEDGEMENTS

With love as always to my two youngest reviewers Arran and Oliver. To Geoff Dobson, Claire, Alice and Yvette, Mum and Dad – with lots of love. Russ and KB Strawson, Dan, June and Jack Stride, Mike, Lynette, William and Henry Edwards, Jay and Anna, for being there to raise a smile when things were tough. Sharla Ault – IAG for words, deeds and encouragement. Caroline D'Subin and of course Leni for the happiness we've shared. Simon Penn, Sid Lalwani, Laxmi and Kayin – without whom I'd never have started. The team at Iniquus – for your patience and tech savvy. Trevor and Jane Mewse, Katharine and Jon Hulls for smiles and happiness, afloat and ashore. Sue Whitfield, Steve, Naimh, Annie and Joshua Dyer – my biggest fans and great friends. Mark Williams, Lisa and Hayden Littlewood for helping me stay sane when everything came crashing down. Della Heath – wishing you happiness come what may. Katie Newell – "you're kidding me!", Jaz, Marcia, Neve and Tia Francis; Dave, Alison and the Harris family; Matt, Clare and the Wells clan – smiles and hugs to Bristol. Vivien Russell for services beyond the call of flight crew. Heather White, wishing for your success – soon! Lynn Forbes, norty lady! Hola Heather, Stuart, Sonny and Lois Burrell, wishing you were next door again. Noelle Murphy for lots of smiles, parsley and pants! Françoise Scheepers, thanks for your faith in me. And thanks as always to Thomas and everyone at Jonglez Publishing.

As well as: Antoine Arnoux, Irène Arrouch, Perry and Coline de Belrepayre, Bertrand, Olivier and Armelle de la Blanchardière and their children, Robin Delaporte, Philippe Desmurger, Denis and Emile Duchêne, Mr and Mrs Esnard, Yann Falquerho, Anne Hourman, Daniel Jegat, Isabelle Mascart, Hervé de Mazerac, Patricia Meneguen, Friedrich Pfeffer, the Piot family, and LO-renzo in particular, Benoît Sautillet, Monsieur and Madame Jacques Thénard, Bruno Tourmen, Linda Tribet, the Troisgros family, Jean-Marc Valverde, Guillaume Wibaux and Sylvie Zucco.

Maps: Jean-Baptiste Neny - Layout Design: Roland Deloi, Romaine Guérin and Valérie Jelger - Layout: Stéphanie Benoit - English Editing: Kimberly Bess and Caroline Lawrence.

Already published